THE REVISED VERSION
EDITED FOR THE USE OF SCHOOLS

T0364318

THE
BOOK OF HOSEA

THE
BOOK OF HOSEA

BY

T. W. CRAFER, D.D.

Warden of the College of Greyladies, and Professor
of Theology and Dean of Queen's College, London

CAMBRIDGE
AT THE UNIVERSITY PRESS
1923

CAMBRIDGE
UNIVERSITY PRESS

University Printing House, Cambridge CB2 8BS, United Kingdom

Published in the United States of America by Cambridge University Press, New York

Cambridge University Press is part of the University of Cambridge.

It furthers the University's mission by disseminating knowledge in the pursuit of education, learning and research at the highest international levels of excellence.

www.cambridge.org
Information on this title: www.cambridge.org/9781107647664

© Cambridge University Press 1923

This publication is in copyright. Subject to statutory exception
and to the provisions of relevant collective licensing agreements,
no reproduction of any part may take place without the written
permission of Cambridge University Press.

First published 1923
First paperback edition 2014

A catalogue record for this publication is available from the British Library

ISBN 978-1-107-64766-4 Paperback

Cambridge University Press has no responsibility for the persistence or accuracy of URLs for external or third-party internet websites referred to in this publication, and does not guarantee that any content on such websites is, or will remain, accurate or appropriate.

PREFACE BY THE GENERAL EDITOR FOR THE OLD TESTAMENT

THE aim of this series of commentaries is to explain the Revised Version for young students, and at the same time to present, in a simple form, the main results of the best scholarship of the day.

The General Editor has confined himself to supervision and suggestion. The writer is, in each case, responsible for the opinions expressed and for the treatment of particular passages.

A. H. McNEILE.

October, 1919.

CONTENTS

INTRODUCTION

§ 1. The History of the Period.

It was once the custom to study the prophetical in the light of the historical books of the Old Testament. The difficult utterances of the former were read in conformity with the simple narratives of the latter. We have now come to realise that the prophets represent living voices of contemporary comment on the period in which they lived; whereas the historical books were compiled centuries later in their present form. The latter do indeed incorporate narratives which date back earlier than the prophets, but these are embedded in a record which looks back to a distant past. This has given a new value to the study of the prophets, as revealing the inner life of their nation from the 8th century B.C. onwards.

But it is necessary to begin with an outline of the history in one's mind, which may be obtained not only from books of the Bible, but also from the records of the great nations by which the chosen people were surrounded, Assyria, Egypt, and Babylon. The giving of approximate dates is meant only as a guide to the sequence of events. The separation of the kingdoms of Israel and Judah had taken place about 940 B.C. The southern kingdom of Judah had remained true to Rehoboam and his descendants, so they had still a prince of the house of David in Uzziah (called in Kings Azariah), who came to the throne about 783 B.C. With the temple at Jerusalem as the centre of their worship, and but little connexion with other nations owing to their isolated position among the hills, away from the caravan route which was a highway of the nations, they had kept themselves comparatively free from the influence of the baser religions and grosser morals of the heathen world around them. But it was otherwise with the ten tribes of the northern kingdom of Israel, who held the more spacious and fertile territory which was traversed by the caravan route which skirted the coast-line from Egypt, and then crossed the plain of Jezreel or Esdraelon, which has been the battleground of the nations as well as their highway.

Not only did they suffer severely from the inroads of their northern neighbour Syria, but they were continually menaced by the two great empires, Egypt in the south-west, and Assyria in the north-east. Moreover they were influenced greatly both in religion and morals by the nations with whom they came in contact, and at one period, during the dynasty of Ahab, various forms of the worship of Baal almost ousted that of Jehovah. But no one dynasty continued in power for long, and successful revolutions were frequent in their history. One of the most important was in about 840 B.C. when Jehu ended the dynasty which had popularised Baal, and destroyed his cult at the same time. In the period that followed, the nation was nominally true to Jehovah as their local God, but the cult of the Golden Calves, which Jeroboam had set up, inclined them to idolatry. Moreover their religion was largely modelled on the grossly immoral cult of Baal and other foreign deities. This meant that there were actually sanctuaries in Israel where, in the name of what they pictured as the creative and productive power of nature, women offered themselves as prostitutes, and men gratified their sinful lusts and called it a religious rite. Such degrading immoralities must be mentioned in order that Hosea's words may be understood, and they help to explain how the century that followed was one of national decay. Yet there soon came a period of great outward prosperity, which really only made things worse. About the same time that Uzziah became king in

Judah, c. 783, there arose the most powerful and successful of all Israel's kings in the person of Jeroboam II. A brief summary of his forty years' reign is found in 2 Kings xiv. 23-29. He extended his borders, ended the continual menace from Syria, and created such a period of commercial prosperity that Amos describes his nobles as lying on beds of ivory and drinking wine in bowls. But the new commercial spirit only brutalised them, and they sought to add to their wealth by dishonesty, injustice and oppression of the poor (Amos vi. 4-6 and viii. 4-6). After the king's death, c. 743, decay led to speedy collapse. His son Zechariah was deposed after a few months by Shallum, but the usurper was at once assassinated by his rival Menahem, who succeeded in remaining on the throne till c. 737, and bequeathing it to his son Pekahiah. But the great king of Assyria, Tiglath-Pileser ('Pul' of 2 Kings xv. 19) was pressing out the life of the nations which resisted his advance, and Menahem only bought a temporary respite from this new menace by paying a heavy tribute. Pekahiah only remained two years on his precarious throne. For he was assassinated in his palace at Samaria by Pekah, one of his captains, who reigned until he was himself assassinated by Hoshea c. 730. But Pekah's policy was worse than Menahem's. He made alliance with Rezin of Syria against the mighty foe advancing to destroy them both, and they both declared war on Judah when that country refused to join the hopeless confederacy. In 734 the blow fell; the Assyrians took Damascus and destroyed Syria, and, after an attack on the northern parts of Israel, deported many of their inhabitants. It was therefore a sorry kingdom which Hoshea seized, and his only hope of safety was to become the vassal of Assyria. But there was still a remote chance that Egypt could be persuaded to come out and fight the rival empire which was drawing so near to her own borders. This would mean that Hoshea was freed from his vassalage. He therefore in c. 725 invited So (or Sabako) of Egypt to his aid, and threw off the Assyrian yoke. But So never came; instead of him, the Assyrian king Shalmaneser arrived before the walls of Samaria, and after a long and hopeless siege the city fell in 721. The population was then deported, and Israel was wiped off the map. The fall of the nation, and its inner causes, is forcibly described in 2 Kings xvii.

Meanwhile Judah likewise nearly fell before Assyria. Uzziah died shortly after his northern contemporary Jeroboam II, and stormy years followed for his successors Jotham and Ahaz. The latter came to the throne in c. 735, about the same time that Pekah seized the northern kingship, and was attacked by the latter because he refused to join him against Assyria. His own policy was to appeal to Tiglath-Pileser for help, in spite of the advice of Isaiah to remain quiet within his Judaean fastnesses. The flood of invasion which swept away Israel in 721 failed to reach as far as Judah, where Hezekiah had succeeded his father Ahaz. It was 20 years later, in 701, that the crisis came for Judah, in the invasion of the Assyrians under Sennacherib, and the siege of Jerusalem. If the nation survived the crisis, and the holy city did not meet the same fate as Samaria, but enjoyed another century of freedom, the cause was in something more than the varying fortune of war, and depended also on the different moral and spiritual conditions of the two kingdoms. It is for this inner side of the history that we turn to the prophets for guidance.

§ 2. THE WORK OF THE PROPHETS—AMOS AND HOSEA.

The work of the prophets in the 8th century B.C. was not a new thing. In the northern kingdom Elijah had witnessed for Jehovah against Baal, and withstood to his face the sinful Ahab. Elisha had had a happier task, and had saved the southern kingdom from a calamity in its war with Moab. But it was not till the time of Jeroboam II that a prophet arose whose words were written down and and are still to be known and read. About the year 760 a man of Judah appeared in the northern kingdom, and uttered a series of denunciations against the hypocritical and profligate conditions which he saw there, with stern warnings that these things were drawing the nation inevitably to punishment and exile. They were outraging the justice of their righteous God, and were sealing their doom thereby. Although these warnings were repeated over a period of several years, their only effect (apart from the stirring of uneasy consciences that must have followed) seems to have been that Amos was warned off as an impudent intruder by the representatives of religion (Amos vii. 10). But he gave to the world a new realisation of a God who was not merely local or national, but was concerned with all the nations of the earth. This God was not simply the protector of His people; on the contrary, the higher their privilege, the greater their responsibility. To worship a God of righteousness was in itself a call to live righteously. Failing this, the day of the Lord, to which they complacently looked forward, would be darkness and not light (Amos v. 18). The stern moralist bore his witness and departed, and in his place arose Hosea, no visitor from the south, but a man of Israel, for whom the condition of his nation was still nearer to his heart. During the ten years beginning about 745 (only a few years after Amos had ceased to warn), Hosea uttered a series, not of mere warnings, but of tender appeals, based not on the righteousness of Jehovah, but on His love. The last chance given to the decadent nation lay in the appeal to them to return to the God whose love they had outraged, and give Him an answering love, which should extend also to their fellowmen. Nothing short of a national repentance would do, and so Hosea the Israelite addresses, not the men and women of Israel, as the prophet from Judah had done, but the nation itself, which he personifies throughout, sometimes calling it by the name of Ephraim, its central and dominant tribe. The two prophets form a complete contrast, and their relation is well worth study[1]. But though the form of their appeal was different, the message itself was the same. 'The religious world has always been divided into men who look at the questions of faith from the standpoint of universal ethics, and men by whom moral truths are habitually approached from a personal sense of the grace of God....But Yahveh chose his prophets from men of both types, and preached the same lesson to Israel through both[2].' But the nation gave heed to neither, and headed straight for moral and religious bankruptcy. A nation that has not lost its soul cannot be wiped off the map by a conquering enemy (Belgium is a modern illustration of this truth). But that is exactly what had happened to Israel, and so, about a dozen years after Hosea's patriotic efforts seem to have ended, it collapsed irrevocably. It was more than the ill-fortune of war; for it had sinned against light, against the Holy Spirit 'Who spake by the prophets.'

§ 3. HOSEA AND HIS MESSAGE.

Although we know nothing about Hosea except from his own words, he appears before us as so attractive, and indeed so pathetic, a personality, that to read the book without learning to know its author is to lose half its interest and meaning. In no other book of the Bible, except the Psalms and perhaps some of S. Paul's Epistles, does the author open to the world in all simplicity his own

---

[1] See Harper, *I.C.C.* pp. cxlv–clv. G. A. Smith, *Expositor's Bible*, pp. 227–231.
[2] W. Robertson Smith, *Prophets of Israel*, p. 163.

throbbing and bleeding heart. The psychologist may like to study and dissect it, but there is something so movingly human in Hosea that all the world may feel their kinship with him, provided that they move on high enough planes of religious emotion. And throughout he is intensely and sometimes painfully practical. Never was a man less separable from his message. First he lived it, and then he spoke it. And so we must consider both him and it in one section, passing in review (a) His personal life, (b) The message which it suggested, (c) His message as a whole.

(a) *His personal life.* In the first three chapters he tells the sad story of his life, and the grievous thing which wrecked his home. He had married a wife named Gomer, and his exquisite description of Jehovah teaching his son Israel to walk, in the infancy of the nation, and holding him by the arms (xi. 3) reveals him as a man in whose life domestic love came first, and we can imagine him with his own little son Jezreel. But the immorality of his day, often indulged in, as we have seen, in the name of religion, was having its inevitable effect on the nation, and causing women as well as men to regard lightly the marriage bond, and seek other lovers. Hosea's own wife proved thus unfaithful, and when a second child was born, he knew that he was not its father, and so he called the fatherless little daughter Lo-ruhamah, 'unpitied,' or 'unloved.' In time another son was born to his 'wife of whoredoms,' whom he called Lo-ammi, 'not my people,' or 'not my kin.' And all the while he refused to divorce or expel his wife. For his tender love for her never ceased, in spite of all the pain, and he hoped she would see at length the error of her ways, and respond to the unfailing appeal of his love. Instead of this, she deserted him for some other man, and followed the inevitable drift of such a life until she was in the position of a slave-concubine. Here was the opportunity for her husband's undying love. He bought her back to him for half the price of a slave, and kept her for a while in his home, not in her former honoured position as the wife of his bosom, but apart, under a gentle restraint, until such time as she realised her sin. It may be that this tragedy of home had no happy ending. Or the husband's unending hope may at length have had its reward, and, accepting the two last children as his own, he took the prefix from their names, and called them Ruhamah, 'pitied', and Ammi, 'my people'. And yet, had this been the case, he would surely have tried to forget the sorrows of the past, and keep them locked in his own breast. But as he utters his message, we find him still in bitter anguish of soul, transferring the private tragedy of his own relation with his unfaithful wife, in order to illustrate by it the public tragedy of his nation, the unfaithful spouse of faithful Jehovah, who would fain draw her back to Himself in love, and be the Father of all her children.

(b) *The message suggested by his personal life.* We do not know how soon Hosea became a prophet. It has been surmised, from his familiarity with the priests and their perverted aims, that he was himself a priest, lamenting the degeneracy of his fellows. But there is no indication that he was one who saw visions, and through them was impelled to give utterance to what he had seen of the mind of God. Nor was he a prophet whose first object was to foretell the horrors which were so speedily to befall his nation. Prophecy was with him more of the New Testament type, an inspired preaching which revealed God to men. So sure was he whence his message came, that he felt no need to preface the divine message, as the other prophets so often did, with 'Thus saith the Lord.' He was doubtless profoundly moved by the preaching of Amos, though to his emotional nature it must have seemed to leave out the highest thing of all, the love that conquers all. But the form of his own message was shaped by his personal experience. As he brooded in silent agony over

the unfaithfulness of his wife, the thought came to him
that the love for her which still burned in his own heart
was like Jehovah's love for unfaithful Israel. When his
first child was born he called him 'Jezreel,' 'God shall
scatter,' in plain reference to the scattering that should
befall his nation. This symbolic name is akin to those
which Isaiah gave his sons (Is. vii. 3 and viii. 1), and indi-
cates that he already felt himself to be a prophet. To the
next children he gives names which may have only been
suggested by their being born to his wife in sin. But Lo-
ruhamah, 'unpitied,' suited equally well the land that had
forfeited the right to God's pity, and 'Lo-ammi' was just
what the fatherly heart of God must feel about the people
who had ceased to be His. And so, in the certainty of his
own undying love as husband and father, there comes to
him, perhaps not a vision, but an intuition of the love of
God to Israel. And as he uses all means to win back his
wife, and awaken her love once more, he feels that, by the
pathetic recital of his own story, he can touch the heart of
his nation, and draw it back to God. But as there must
come a time of punishment and probation first, he realises
that, just as he keeps his wife in solitude for a while,
waiting patiently for the change to come in her which alone
can make the restoration complete, so God must send
Israel into exile, to await a full restoration which must
depend upon herself. We have said that it is doubtful
whether his wife had responded when he spoke his message.
Did he expect a restoration of Israel after its fall? The
answer to this is to be found in the final prophecy of his
book (ch. xiv.) where Ephraim puts away idols and delights
to be 'like a green fir tree,' and Jehovah assures his restored people 'from me is thy fruit found.' But some critics
regard ch. xiv. as an addition to the book made by some
later hand. This must be discussed later (*infra*, pp. 19, 20),
but it is enough to say here that, even if that last prophecy

be set aside, it is difficult to think that he can have placed his God below himself in the lastingness of his hopeful and expectant love.

This message, which occupies the first three chapters of his book, seems to have been uttered while Jeroboam was still on the throne, in the years preceding 743. An indication of this is found in his prediction that the blood of Jezreel (where Ahab was killed by Jehu) should be avenged 'upon the house of Jehu' (i. 4). For Jeroboam (whose dynasty ended with the murder of his son Zechariah after a reign of only a few months) was evidently still reigning. The prophet gives this as the reason why he called his own son 'Jezreel.' The rest of his book evidently dates from the period of anarchy and rapid decline which followed the first of a series of usurpations six months after Jeroboam's death. In these later prophecies he makes no further reference to his own domestic experience. But, though the message is no longer conveyed by such picturesque means, the tone and attitude are the same throughout.

(c) *The prophet's message as a whole.* Hosea judges his people's needs by the contrast which he saw between the character and demands of God, in his own mind, and in the thought and practice of the nation. Reference should therefore be made to the following paragraph (§ 4) on his theology and religious ideas. He felt that the only chance for this decadent Israel, which had lost the knowledge of God, was in a complete change of attitude and of life. Their ignorance of God's real character had led them into three things: (1) a corrupted worship of Jehovah, which copied the gross immoralities of Canaanitish heathenism; (2) a state of political anarchy, which made them turn to one usurping king after another; (3) a weak and hesitating foreign policy, which made them put their faith in some great alliance, without being able to agree whether it should be with Assyria or Egypt. The same sin was at

the back of all three, an unfaithfulness which shewed itself
in their desertion of the true worship of God, and in a lack
of trust which made them turn to earthly kings instead of
to the Heavenly King, and trust to world powers instead of
seeking fuller alliance with the power of God. To the nation
thus in decay both morally and politically he proclaims a
message of certain disaster, unless they truly repent. As
they learnt of God in the wilderness of the Exodus, so
a fresh discipline awaited them in the wilderness of the
Exile. Their only hope of avoiding extinction lay in a real
national repentance. If only they make it, then the God
whose love they had outraged and whose faithfulness
they had flaunted would welcome them back, like the
prodigal son, to the bosom of the Father's love.

§ 4. Hosea's Theology and Religious Ideas.

(*a*) The real importance of Hosea lies in his revelation
that '*God is love.*' To the Christian it is an old truism, but
to Israel in the 8th century B.C. it was a new truth. Amos
had already revealed the fact that Jehovah was no mere
tribal or national God, interested only in the soil of Palestine, and not concerned with the world around. It was left
to Isaiah and his successors to deny the existence of any
other God, and to set forth the one God as using all nations
for the working out of His purpose. It is true that Hosea
represents Jehovah both as Maker and Upholder, but these
things have not the chief prominence in his theology. His
quarrel with belief in local Baals and in the debasing
worship of them is not so much because they are impossible
rivals of the true God, as because He is a spiritual God,
and if His worship is mixed with the unspiritual worship of
other cults, it is an outrage on His love, in gross ignorance
of His true character.

But he speaks, not as trying to uplift his nation to a

higher religion which was only now being evolved from the lower thoughts and experiences of the past. The religion he preaches is before all things 'historic,' and rooted in the past. He points back to Jacob, the ancestor and namesake of Israel, and to his early experiences of God's fatherly care. He shews that at the birth of the nation at the Exodus, God's people had already become His beloved son, in whom He was well pleased. Their history was a growing manifestation of His faithfulness, which remained just as true and tender in spite of their own unfaithfulness.

Although his painful duty was to give stern and hopeless warning, his religious outlook still contained bright flashes of hope in a glorious future, in which God was yearning to do His part if only man would do his own. The gloom of the present and the punishment that lay straight before his nation were signs, not of divine wrath, but of fatherly correction which was meant for their good.

And further, it is from God's point of view and not man's that he expounds his theology. It was his own painful domestic experience and the yearning of his disappointed heart, which brought him to the knowledge of the Divine character. The supreme appeal is from a tender heart which he dares to think of as that of a husband, feeling for Israel just what S. Paul pictures our Lord as feeling for 'His spouse the Church,' loving and cherishing it, and longing for it to be without 'spot or wrinkle or any such thing' (Eph. vi. 27). And even as his own heart yearned over children as well as wife, so did he see his God as the Father as well as the Husband of His people. Jehovah had 'taught Ephraim to go,' as a father teaches his baby child to walk, rejoicing over them, looking for their filial response, and (xi. 3) never despairing that even the prodigal son would some day 'come to himself,' and arise and go to his Father. Sometimes the prophet is overcome by the gulf that separates God from man, as wide as that between man and beast.

It is then that he recalls his experience as a man, not of the town, but of the country; for he compares God to the merciful man who is merciful to his beast (xi. 4), and yet who has to make his oxen work, and to put the yoke on the neck of an obstinate heifer (x. 11). Perhaps the chief value of the study of Hosea's book is to learn afresh from a living, loving, yearning heart of long ago the fatherly tenderness of the God with whom we have to do.

(*b*) A few words must be said about *man as the object of God's love*. Hosea confines his thought to his own nation, but within those limits it is strange to find that he has no message for the individual soul. He deals with Israel throughout as a solid whole. Even when classes in the community come within his view, priests and prophets, kings and princes, there is no separate dealing. The religious unit is the community, which is personified throughout, in a solidarity alike of guilt, of punishment and of subsequent restoration as the result of repentance. This does not mean that there is no lesson for the Christian, who has learnt the infinite worth of the individual soul in the Divine love and purpose. The very fact that Hosea uses his own personal experience to lead himself and his hearers to God, encourages us to read between the lines a personal message. But such stress has come to be laid on the individualistic side of religion, that a needed lesson is contained in the teaching of a nation's solidarity in moral responsibility and in repentance as a condition of acceptance. In this Hosea speaks direct to the 20th century. And again, with many of us the conception of the 'Holy Catholic Church' is so shadowy that our oneness in God's sight as a religious community requires a new stress. It is here that Pusey's commentary on the book is not out of date, and the more so because this is not a line of thought which has appealed to commentators since his day.

(*c*) From the standpoint of the religious life, the book still affords a real contribution towards the working out of the great themes of *sin, repentance, and forgiveness*. Hosea has been styled 'the first preacher of repentance' (see the chapters on 'Repentance,' and 'The Sin against Love' in G. A. Smith's *Twelve Prophets*, pp. 333–354). And yet it is possible to say 'It has scarcely ever been found either necessary to add to the terms which Hosea used for repentance, or possible to go deeper in analysing the processes which these denote.' Sin is revealed as consisting, not only in specific acts of wrong which anger God, but in attitudes of heart and life which grieve Him. Repentance is something far more than the confident repetition of a beautiful form of words, but when the words mean a real Godward turning of the life, forgiveness is certain, even though correction must come before restoration, as a part of what God knows to be needful. And such a forgiveness, with repentance as its condition, may be freely proclaimed by God's representative, in His Name.

(*d*) A final word on the subject of *worship*. If Hosea proclaims that 'God is a Spirit,' in contrast with the debased ideas of an Israel tainted with the gross and material cults of Canaan, the natural exhortation he gives is to 'worship him in spirit and in truth.' Perhaps the most familiar sentence in his book, sanctified by its double use in S. Matthew's Gospel (ix. 13 and xii. 7), is 'I desire mercy (or "leal love") and not sacrifice' (vi. 6). An attractive theory put forward by some recent critics is that the prophets were entirely against all forms of animal sacrifice, and that all the passages which depreciate the outward ceremonial connected with traditional Jewish worship (e.g. Amos v. 21–23 and Is. l. 11) are aimed against the whole system. In the case of some of the prophets (and Hosea among them) the Protestant instinct of many commentators has been to contrast the prophetic ideal of spiritual worship with the priestly ritual of the sacrificial system. If this is a passing tendency of criticism, no stress should be laid upon it. Nowhere does Hosea denounce the worship of sacrificial altars and high places as wrong in itself. He agrees with the other prophets in seeing that outward and mechanical worship is useless without an inward effort of the heart. But what he declares to be the sin of Israel is the corruption of national worship by introducing heathen elements into it from the cults of the land, and addressing it to Jehovah only in name. The calves set up by Jeroboam are naturally denounced, and so is the worship connected with pillars, trees, and the like. The Canaanitish cults were connected with gross immoralities. As the various forms of Baal were regarded as the local gods which made the land fertile when duly placated, women were encouraged to offer themselves to sexual sin with that object in view, and a 'spirit of whoredom' in the national life was the result. The moral standard of the nation was thus lowered, and there was an inner sense in which it became unfaithful to its true husband Jehovah, by seeking other forms of deity as its paramours. The sanctuaries of the land, Beth-el, Gilgal, and the rest, had thus become the centres not of uplifting but of degrading influence. On this many of the picturesque but terrible utterances of Hosea are based. The nation had become adulterous in a double sense, and paid the penalty accordingly. Their literal adultery, which they even sought to justify in the name of religion, led to inchastity in home-life, and the national menace of a falling birth-rate. And their spiritual adultery alienated them from their God, and deadened their ears to the cry of His prophet, with the result that they sinned away their final opportunity, which was offered them in his impassioned appeal to repent and be saved.

§ 5. THE RELATION OF THE BOOK TO THE REST OF THE OLD TESTAMENT.

Among the assured results of modern criticism may be ranked the placing of the earlier prophetical books at a date long before the other books, including those of the Law, assumed their present final form. If Amos has thus become the earliest complete book of the Old Testament, Hosea stands second. It is true that the most primitive of the elements which make up the composite narrative from the beginning of Genesis onwards, the Judaean or Jehovistic code, probably dates from the 8th century B.C., but it was only one of several sources which make up the so-called Pentateuch. Thus Hosea must not be read as reflecting the early narratives and traditions which we possess in the Bible, but as in some sense anticipating them. Three interesting conclusions may be arrived at: (1) Hosea knows of a *torah* or law of God already in existence for a long period, which the nation has once known and heeded ('Thou hast forgotten the law of thy God,' iv. 6), and seemingly used in a written form ('Though I write for him my law in ten thousand precepts,' viii. 12). (2) This law is rather moral than ceremonial, for it stands in contrast with mere sacrifices (viii. 13). (3) The law which Hosea knows corresponds with that of the Book of the Covenant (Exod. xx.–xxiii.), and although his warnings concerning disobedience, etc. are somewhat in the spirit of Deuteronomy, there is every indication that he lived long before that book was written, for he has no idea of the centralisation of worship in Jerusalem, nor of the sin of worship as such in various sanctuaries and high-places.

When we turn from laws to narratives, the most notable feature is Hosea's independence of the Biblical accounts and particularly of the writer's estimates of them. Thus, while the story of Jacob (xii. 3, 4, 5, 12) substantially agrees with Genesis, the incident of Peniel is placed before that of Beth-el (xii. 4), and a lesson is drawn from the deceitful side of the patriarch's character (xii. 7).

The same bold treatment is found in relation to the later history. The unsavoury story of Gibeah and the Benjamites (Judges xix.) is somewhat strangely singled out as a mark of the beginning of Israel's decay. And although the narrative of Kings shews that the usurpation of Jeroboam had the encouragement of God through His prophet, Hosea (according to one interpretation of viii. 4), dates from his act the national apostasy. And again the act of Jehu in exterminating the house of Ahab is regarded by him in so novel a light that he declares that God will 'avenge the blood of Jezreel' (where his triumph over Jehoram and Baal-worship took place) 'upon the house of Jehu' (i. 4).

There is at least one passage where he seems to echo the words of Amos, but on the whole his thought and language is singularly independent of his elder contemporary.

Another line of comparison is between Hosea and later prophets. This has been given a new interest by Melville Scott (*The Message of Hosea*, pp. 89–102). He collects parallels with Jeremiah, including both theological resemblances and actual parallels such as Jer. xiv. 10, which seems a literal transcript of Hosea viii. 13 (repeated in ix. 9 as the refrain of the sentence). He proceeds to argue that Jeremiah, as 'the spiritual heir of Hosea,' was drawn to him because he proclaimed, like himself, a double message of doom and restoration, thus disproving the recent radical treatment of Hosea, which would relegate to a later interpolator all the passages which give hope of restoration. The likenesses between Hosea and Ezekiel may be used in the same way.

§ 6. THE STYLE, TEXT, AND INTEGRITY OF THE BOOK.

S. Jerome's famous summary of Hosea's style is 'Osee commaticus est,' i.e. broken up into clauses. He passes from one thought to another with strange abruptness, and, perhaps owing to the conflicting emotions within him which confused the utterance of his message, 'each verse forms a whole for itself, like one heavy toll in a funeral knell' (Pusey). He harps on the same theme without monotony, and his bold and suggestive figures reveal him as a man of the open air, with first-hand knowledge of lions and heifers, of rains and night-mists, of flowers and tree-roots and the slopes of Lebanon. His style may be spoken of as classical Hebrew, and its poetic element has always been recognised. But it is only of late years that his utterances have been divided into a series of lyrical strophes, consisting of some eight to twelve lines apiece. There seems little doubt that any elaborate or artificial arrangement of the kind can easily be exaggerated, especially when theories are built upon it, such as the alteration of the text and occasional omission of parts of it because the strophic regularity seems to be broken. Harper (*International Critical Commentary*, p. clxix) claims that difficult passages may thus be eliminated. But when he proceeds to omit those passages which interfere with his theory that the original Hosea gave no message of restoration, it is difficult to follow him.

The text is one of the most corrupt in the Old Testament, and its obscurities have given rise to endless emendations, many of them without the least support from any text or version. The corruption of the text had already begun when the Septuagint version was made, for it shares many of the difficulties of the Hebrew. But there are many places where it seems to give the clue to the right reading, and this has been noted in a number of instances in the commentary which follows.

The book was formerly accepted by all as coming from Hosea himself, his utterances having probably been compiled by his own hand near the close of his life. But modern criticism has changed this view, and editors have made Hosea say just as much as they think he ought to have said, and no more, by the theory that the book was compiled at a much later date, and is full of glosses and interpolations which date from the exile and after it. Two difficulties in particular have been thus treated : (1) Interwoven with the message to the northern kingdom of Israel, there comes the occasional mention of the southern kingdom along with it. It is proposed either to remove the clauses which contain the word 'Judah,' or to substitute 'Israel' for it. There is certainly one place (xii. 2) where the latter course seems justifiable and another (i. 7) which suggests the former, but on the whole there seems no more reason for thinking that Hosea the Israelite would not deal with Judaean interests than that Isaiah of Judah should have nothing to say to Israel. (2) A far more important question is whether the book is to be levelled down to a consistent prediction of doom, with no hint of divine forgiveness when the penalty of sin has been paid ; or whether the hope of restoration is to be seen running through the book like a silver thread, and shining out at length in the glorious picture of the reconciliation of faithful Jehovah and his faithless people in the last chapter.

The former course is followed by Harper (*op. cit.* see espec. pp. clix ff.) although much of the spiritual meaning of the book is ruined thereby. Melville Scott's book *The Message of Hosea* is specially aimed at overthrowing such a view. It is impossible to discuss the question here, but in support of the integrity of the book and the gospel of hope as preached by Hosea, it may be urged, among many other considerations, (1) that it would be monstrous for the prophet to have hope for his own erring wife to the end, and yet declare that God had finally flung off faithless Israel, whether they repented or not; (2) that ch. xiv. shews no change in style, and is one of the most exquisite passages in the book, and yet its tender promise would have to be ascribed to some later editor or interpolator.

It may be added that the question is not affected by the likelihood that the closing words of hope in the book of Amos may be a later addition. But it must not be thought that, because ruthless and drastic treatment of the text of Hosea does not seem more than a passing phase of criticism, the text must therefore be left as it is. Many ingenious and often convincing emendations have been suggested, and all the important ones will receive attention. Nor is it unreasonable, in the case of a text so corrupt, to suppose an occasional dislocation in the order, as in the case of chs. ii. and iii., or of *v.* 12 of ch. ix. (see notes).

It is exceedingly difficult to find many obvious divisions in so disjointed a book. The one thing clear is that chs. i.–iii. stand apart from the rest. Some find as many as thirteen separate prophecies in the chapters which follow. The present writer has suggested a form of division which probably is purely accidental, but may be worth mentioning, if only as an answer to the claim to have discovered an elaborate division of the book into strophes. All the main divisions of the book will be found to consist of multiples of 13 verses. The first main division is chs. i.–iii., making 39 verses. In the long section iv.–x., each of the two main divisions consists of 52 verses, viz. iv. 1–vii. 8 and vii. 9–x. 15. The last four chapters of the book, which stand apart from what precedes, also consist of 52 verses, or rather 51, but the double form of the concluding verse, which is in the nature of an epilogue, suggests that it may be counted as two. Again, these four chapters may be naturally subdivided thus : xi.–xii. 1, 13 verses : xii. 2–14, 13 verses (or xi. and xii. together, 26 verses); xiii. 1–xiv. 9, 26 (25) verses. In the summary which follows, sections were made as above before the thought of artificial divisions had suggested itself. Recent criticism, in denying the integrity of the book, has claimed that some sections and a number of separate verses are to be regarded as later additions, because they spoil either the consistency of Hosea's attitude or the symmetry of his strophes. Would it not be also possible to claim that not a single verse must be omitted, because it would spoil the arithmetical system which runs through the book? (For a summary of recent criticism, see Art. in *Ch. Quart. Rev.* for Jan. 1923, 'Modern Criticism and the Prophetic Literature of the Old Testament,' by T. H. Robinson.)

§ 7. SUMMARY OF HOSEA'S PROPHECIES.

I. The first prophecy, belonging to the latter part of Jeroboam II's reign (c. 750–743 B.C.). The Prophet's love for his unfaithful wife illustrates God's love for unfaithful Israel. i. 2–iii. 5.

II. A series of prophecies, in the time of increasing moral and political collapse which followed Jeroboam II's death (c. 743–735 B.C.). iv. 1–xiv. 9.

A. Israel's moral decay and its sequel. iv. 1–vii. 7.
  1. Jehovah's condemnation of the corrupted nation. iv.
  2. Jehovah's condemnation of the priests and princes. v. 1–14.
  3. Jehovah will not spare unless repentance is real. v. 15–vii. 2.
  4. Their kings are involved in the general degradation. vii. 3–7.

B. Israel's political decay and its sequel. vii. 8–x. 15.
  1. Israel's foolish foreign policy. vii. 8–viii. 3.
  2. The futility of setting up kings and making gods. viii. 4–ix. 17.
  3. A summary of their sins, which are leading them to despair and to punishment. x. 1–10.
  4. Jehovah's yoke was heavier than they thought. x. 11–15.

C. The penalty of ignoring the fatherly love of God. xi. 1–xii. 1.

D. In their deceit they are like their father Jacob, whose history is a lesson for the present. xii. 2–14.

E. The last judgement of Israel. xiii. 1–16.

F. God's love triumphs, in a new covenant with His people. xiv.

§ 8. THE USE OF HOSEA IN THE NEW TESTAMENT.

Hosea i. 10. *Rom.* ix. 25. (In proof of the call of the Gentiles.)

Hosea i. 10 and 23. 1 *Pet.* ii. 10. (Of the call of Christians to be 'a holy nation, a people for God's own possession.')

Hosea vi. 6. *S. Matth.* ix. 13. (Our Lord's rebuke to the Pharisees when they complained that He ate with sinners.) *S. Matth.* xii. 7. (When the Pharisees complained that the disciples had plucked corn on the Sabbath day.)

Hosea x. 8. *S. Luke* xxiii. 30. (Our Lord's prediction to the daughters of Jerusalem.) *Rev.* vi. 16. (Of the 'great day' when the sixth seal is opened.)

Hosea xi. 1. *S. Matth.* ii. 15. (Of the flight into Egypt from Herod.)

Hosea xiii. 14. 1 *Cor.* xv. 55. (Of the victory over death in the resurrection.)

THE
BOOK OF HOSEA

i. i. THE TITLE.

The word of the LORD that came unto Hosea the son 1
of Beeri, in the days of Uzziah, Jotham, Ahaz, and Hezekiah, kings of Judah, and in the days of Jeroboam the son
of Joash, king of Israel.

---

i. 1. This verse simply introduces the prophecies, and must be
by a later hand. It is better to trust to the other references in the
book, for the date here given is not a consistent one. **The days
of Jeroboam** only reached to 743 B.C., but the *days of Hezekiah*
as king of Judah only began c. 727 B.C. There is nothing in the
prophecies which seems to date from as late as 734 B.C., when
Israel and Syria allied against Assyria, and went to war with
Judah because they refused to join them. If the prophet's work
was within some such limits as 750–735, it would be in the reigns
of Jeroboam II, Zechariah, Shallum, Menahem, Pekahiah and
Pekah in the north, and Uzziah (or Azariah), Jotham and
Ahaz in the south.

The word of the Lord. 'LORD' thus printed represents the
sacred name *Yahweh*, which came to be written Jehovah.

Hosea. The name is the same as that of Hoshea, the last king
of Israel, and is also the original form of Joshua. Its meaning is
'Salvation.'

the son of Beeri. To identify this man with Beerah, the
Reubenite prince of 1 Chron. v. 6, is a mere guess, though an
ancient one. All we can say about the family is that they must
have been country folk, for Hosea loves to talk of cornfields, of
oxen at work, and the like. If he was a countryman like Amos,
he probably also followed the 'father of written prophecy' in
not being a prophet's son. But the suggestion that he was a
priest is not an unlikely one, for he speaks with familiarity of
holy things, and evidently had always been of a deeply religious
bent.

I. The Prophet's love for his unfaithful wife
illustrates God's love for unfaithful Israel.
i. 2–iii. 5.

i. 2–ii. 1. *The story of his unfaithful wife
and bastard children.*

2 When the Lord spake at the first by Hosea, the Lord
said unto Hosea, Go, take unto thee a wife of whoredom
and children of whoredom: for the land doth commit great
3 whoredom, departing from the Lord. So he went and
took Gomer the daughter of Diblaim; and she conceived,
4 and bare him a son. And the Lord said unto him, Call
his name Jezreel; for yet a little while, and I will avenge

---

2. the Lord said. It was only afterwards that he realised that
his domestic misfortune could be thus used as part of his
prophetic message.

a wife of whoredom. There is no need to think that he pur-
posely married a bad woman, or that she had acted immorally
before marriage. It was only after marriage that the taint of
impurity manifested itself.

children of whoredom. It was not till the first child had
been born that he discovered it was not his own.

the land doth commit great whoredom. He applies his story
as he narrates the stages of it. Throughout his prophecies he
regards the sinful people of Israel as one individual, the chosen
spouse of Jehovah, **the land** personified. He has no separate
messages, like Amos, for the various people and classes that
constitute the state. Israel had once been as a chaste maiden,
until her **departing from the Lord.**

3. Gomer the daughter of Diblaim. The suggestion that the
whole story is merely an allegory is made the more unlikely by
the fact that these names have no symbolical reference.

4. Call his name Jezreel: that is, 'God sows,' or 'God will
scatter.' The name symbolises the scattering that is to come,
when Jeroboam II shall die and his son soon after him, and the
dynasty of Jehu shall be at an end.

I will avenge the blood of Jezreel. He looks backward as
well as forward. It was in the valley of Jezreel that Jehu had
slain the house of Ahab. For Hosea's condemnation of Jehu's act,
which is quite unlike the attitude of 2 Kings x. 11, see Introd.
p. 17, and note on viii. 4.

the blood of Jezreel upon the house of Jehu, and will cause
the kingdom of the house of Israel to cease. And it shall 5
come to pass at that day, that I will break the bow of
Israel in the valley of Jezreel. And she conceived again, 6
and bare a daughter. And *the LORD* said unto him, Call
her name Lo-ruhamah: for I will no more have mercy
upon the house of Israel, that I should in any wise pardon
them. But I will have mercy upon the house of Judah, 7
and will save them by the LORD their God, and will not
save them by bow, nor by sword, nor by battle, by horses,
nor by horsemen. Now when she had weaned Lo-ruhamah, 8
she conceived, and bare a son. And *the LORD* said, Call 9
his name Lo-ammi: for ye are not my people, and I will
not be your *God*.

---

will cause the kingdom of the house of Israel to cease.
Although it lingered for more than 20 years after Jeroboam's
death, the prophet was right in thinking that the one event
would soon be followed by the other.

5. will break the bow, i.e. cause the defeat.

in the valley of Jezreel. In all ages, from Deborah to Allenby,
the plain of Esdraelon has been a favourite battlefield, and
therefore would be a likely spot for the crushing of Israel.

6. Lo-ruhamah: i.e. 'not-pitied,' or 'not-loved,' signifying in
the case of Israel that God's mercy in sparing the unfaithful nation
could go no further. But as applied to Gomer's daughter, it reveals
her as a bastard, born without a father's love.

7. This verse is the first of a number of passages relating to
Judah which have been regarded as later interpolations in
Hosea's prophecies. There is no need to exclude all reference to
the southern kingdom, which shared the danger that overwhelmed
the northern. Each passage must be considered on its merits.
But this one (1) is a useless interruption of the story; (2) seems
to refer to the miraculous deliverance of Jerusalem from
Sennacherib when beseiged in 701 B.C., in the reign of Hezekiah,
when the 'angel of the Lord' (probably a pestilence) caused the
Assyrians to retreat in panic (2 Kings xix. 35).

8. when she had weaned Lo-ruhamah: i.e. after about three
years, according to Eastern custom. This would suggest the
lapse of some six years between the birth of her first child and
her last.

9. Lo-ammi: i.e. 'not my people.' Here Israel is finally

10   Yet the number of the children of Israel shall be as the sand of the sea, which cannot be measured nor numbered; and it shall come to pass that, in the place where it was

---

shewn to be rejected of God. But it is also Hosea's repudiation of fatherhood in the case of this second son, as 'not my kin.'

It will be noted that the births of the children mark stages in the rejection of Israel. We can imagine the stir created by his story in a nation which still complacently ascribed its prosperity to the God of the land.

10, 11–ii. 1. These three verses form one utterance, and in Hebrew all belong to ch. ii. The passage is one of the most disputed in the book, and appears to be either out of place, or a later interpolation. The four chief theories about it may be summarised thus.

(i) The verses are to be left as they are, and the strangely abrupt transition from rejection to restoration is to be explained by Hosea's disjointed style.

(ii) Omit the verses altogether, as a later addition to the book. But this still leaves no connexion between i. 9 and ii. 2.

(iii) Place the verses at the end of ch. ii., where they form a climax to the promises there contained.

(iv) Insert ch. iii. after i. 9. For an exposition of this solution see Melville Scott, *The Message of Hosea*, pp. 24–39. There are many advantages in this theory. The story is not interrupted, but after the birth of the children in ch. i. a new message comes (iii. 1) 'Go yet, love a woman, etc.'; and he proceeds to buy her back to him after her adultery with a hope that she will love him as a wife again, typifying the hope that 'the children of Israel shall return, and seek the LORD...and shall come with fear unto the LORD and to his goodness in the latter days' (iii. 5). The promise of i. 10–ii. 1 now naturally follows, i.e. that 'the number of the children of Israel shall be as the sand of the sea,' and the children's names shall be changed to a happier significance, the last two becoming 'Ammi,' 'my people,' and 'Ruhamah,' 'pitied.' The children are then naturally represented as being bidden 'plead with your mother' (ii. 2), that she may, through disillusionment and discipline, reach a final repentance, after which the marriage can again be renewed. This represents the contents of ch. ii., which ends with the final promise, based on the children's names, when 'I will say to them which were not my people, Thou art my people; and they shall say, Thou art my God.' With these words the first message of chs. i.–iii. fittingly ends.

said unto them, Ye are not my people, it shall be said unto them, *Ye are* the sons of the living God. And the 11 children of Judah and the children of Israel shall be gathered together, and they shall appoint themselves one head, and shall go up from the land : for great shall be the day of Jezreel. Say ye unto your brethren, Ammi ; and 2 to your sisters, Ruhamah.

ii. 2–5. *Israel is warned of the results of her unfaithfulness.*

Plead with your mother, plead ; for she is not my wife, 2 neither am I her husband : and let her put away her whoredoms from her face, and her adulteries from between her

---

There is so much corruption in the text of the chapters which follow, that this dislocation in the earlier chapters can easily be imagined. If in this commentary the old order is retained, the new must also be borne in mind.

10. in the place where it was said unto them : It is doubtful whether this means their own land, or the land of their captivity. The difficulty is avoided in the less literal rendering of the R.V. mg. 'instead of that which was said.'

the living God : in contrast with the dead idol-gods under whose fatherhood they had placed themselves.

11. The joining of the divided kingdoms after their restoration seems to imply the scattering of Judah as well as Israel, which would place these words after 586 B.C. But if Jeremiah could prophesy the reunion before the exile took place (iii. 18), it is not impossible that Hosea should do the same.

great shall be the day of Jezreel : i.e. 'God sows' shall no more mean a scattering, but Gomer's first son shall typify a scattering of their enemies and the sowing of a joint harvest for the re-united nations.

ii. 1. By the omission of a 'not,' the meaning of the ominous names is now reversed. The sense is echoed in the last verse of ch. ii.

2. Plead with your mother, i.e. God begs the individual Israelites (perhaps Hosea, and his brother-prophets) to plead with the nation as a whole. In this chapter Hosea's private sorrow gives place to the greater sorrow of Jehovah.

her whoredoms : i.e. the Baal worship of v. 13, and the idols and the 'calf of Samaria' of viii. 5 and 6.

3 breasts; lest I strip her naked, and set her as in the day
that she was born, and make her as a wilderness, and set
4 her like a dry land, and slay her with thirst; yea, upon
her children will I have no mercy; for they be children of
5 whoredom. For their mother hath played the harlot: she
that conceived them hath done shamefully: for she said,
I will go after my lovers, that give me my bread and my
water, my wool and my flax, mine oil and my drink.

6-13. *Israel will be disillusioned and disciplined.*

6 Therefore, behold, I will hedge up thy way with thorns,
and I will make a fence against her, that she shall not find
7 her paths. And she shall follow after her lovers, but she
shall not overtake them; and she shall seek them, but shall
not find them: then shall she say, I will go and return to my
8 first husband; for then was it better with me than now. For
she did not know that I gave her the corn, and the wine, and
the oil, and multiplied unto her silver and gold, which they
9 used for Baal. Therefore will I take back my corn in the
time thereof, and my wine in the season thereof, and will
pluck away my wool and my flax which should have covered

---

3. strip her naked. The usual punishment of an adulteress
is here made to express the depopulation and desolation of the
soil.

5. my lovers, i.e. the various forms of Canaanitish worship
which had influenced and corrupted the nation's nominal allegiance
to Jehovah. The gods of the country were regarded as providing
the produce of the soil.

6-7. The Prodigal Wife of the Old Testament shall have the
same experience as the Prodigal Son of the New, who 'came to
himself' when he 'began to be in want,' as the inevitable sequel
of his sins.

8. They had not realised that the blessings which they imagined to come from Baal were really the gifts of Jehovah's love.
So they had actually used some of them to make thankofferings
(and perhaps images) to Baal.

9. Israel should learn again whence these material blessings
really came, by being deprived of them by Jehovah.

her nakedness. And now will I discover her lewdness in 10
the sight of her lovers, and none shall deliver her out of
mine hand. I will also cause all her mirth to cease, her feasts, 11
her new moons, and her sabbaths, and all her solemn assem-
blies. And I will lay waste her vines and her fig trees, 12
whereof she hath said, These are my hire that my lovers
have given me: and I will make them a forest, and the
beasts of the field shall eat them. And I will visit upon 13
her the days of the Baalim, unto which she burned incense;
when she decked herself with her earrings and her jewels,
and went after her lovers, and forgat me, saith the LORD.

14-23. *Discipline and Repentance will lead to Restoration and a second Betrothal.*

Therefore, behold, I will allure her, and bring her into the 14
wilderness, and speak comfortably unto her. And I will 15
give her her vineyards from thence, and the valley of Achor

10-12. The ceasing alike of prosperity and worship implies
more than the natural calamities of bad harvests, etc., and suggests
the coming exile.

11. her new moons. For this festival cf. Amos viii. 5.

13. the days of the Baalim: i.e. the days when she worshipped
the various local Baals. The corrupted worship was directed towards a plurality of gods, as suggested by the heathen nations round,
even though the 'high places' were still nominally for the cult of
Jehovah.

when she decked herself. Ornaments were a customary
adjunct of feminine worship (cf. Exod. iii. 21, 22).

14-18. The discipline of the exile will lead to a new and
restored relation with her true husband. But repentance must
come first and final renunciation of perverted worship.

14. This stage corresponds with Hosea's own action in buying
back Gomer and keeping her for a while in isolation.

into the wilderness: i.e. the exile. But there is also the
thought of that first wilderness through which Israel was once
led from the bondage of Egypt, when she first became the spouse
of Jehovah.

speak comfortably: Heb. speak to her heart. Cf. the words
of the prophet of Judah's return from exile, ' Speak ye comfortably
to Jerusalem' (Is. xl. 2).

15. from thence: i.e. after passing through the wilderness.

for a door of hope: and she shall make answer there, as
in the days of her youth, and as in the day when she came
16 up out of the land of Egypt. And it shall be at that day,
saith the LORD, that thou shalt call me Ishi; and shalt
17 call me no more Baali. For I will take away the names of
the Baalim out of her mouth, and they shall no more be
18 mentioned by their name. And in that day will I make a
covenant for them with the beasts of the field, and with
the fowls of heaven, and with the creeping things of the
ground: and I will break the bow and the sword and the
battle out of the land, and will make them to lie down
19 safely. And I will betroth thee unto me for ever; yea, I
will betroth thee unto me in righteousness, and in judge-
20 ment, and in lovingkindness, and in mercies. I will even
betroth thee unto me in faithfulness: and thou shalt know

---

the valley of Achor: a place of sad memory just after the
wanderings from Egypt had been fulfilled, for it was here that
Achan was stoned (Josh. vii. 24). But although the place meant
'trouble,' it was where sin was put away, and so it opened up a
new hope. Hosea's promise is repeated in Is. lxv. 10.

make answer: i.e. respond to Jehovah's love. Note the
repetition of the word in *v.* 21.

16. Israel has been treating Jehovah as if He were one of the
many forms of Baal. Now, instead of 'Baal,' (her lord and
master), she shall treat Him as 'my Husband.' Many regard this
verse as a gloss on *v.* 19, both on metrical grounds, and from the
way it begins, suggesting a prophetic 'tag.'

17. the names of the Baalim. Many Israelitish names were
compounds of 'Baal,' and it is significant that Ish-Baal was afterwards changed into Ish-bosheth (man of shame).

18. It must be remembered that there was a constant menace
from wild beasts, as well as from hostile neighbours.

19–20. The new betrothal is made impressive by the threefold
repetition of the word. Some commentators have seen in it a
type of the betrothal of the Church and her members to Christ,
by the repetition of the threefold name in Baptism. In any case
we are led to S. Paul's metaphor of the mystical union which is
betwixt Christ and His Church (see Eph. v. 22–27). The qualities
here mentioned are the espousals gifts of Jehovah to His bride.
Faithfulness is His unfailing attribute, as is often re-echoed by
S. Paul.

the LORD. And it shall come to pass in that day, I will 21
answer, saith the LORD, I will answer the heavens, and
they shall answer the earth; and the earth shall answer 22
the corn, and the wine, and the oil; and they shall answer
Jezreel. And I will sow her unto me in the earth; and I 23
will have mercy upon her that had not obtained mercy;
and I will say to them which were not my people, Thou
art my people; and they shall say, *Thou art* my God.

iii. 1-5. *The last scene of the prophet's domestic story.*

And the LORD said unto me, Go yet, love a woman be- 3
loved of *her* friend and an adulteress, even as the LORD
loveth the children of Israel, though they turn unto other

---

21. This final promise begins with the same suspicious tag as
v. 16. Harper (*I. C. C.*) regards all the verses 16-23, except 18-19,
as later than Hosea. Jehovah's gifts are mediated through the
rain from heaven to the fruitful earth, and thence from the crops
that spring from it to the nation that enjoys them. Each is
thought of as asking for what it needs, and getting a response by
God's gift.

22. they shall answer Jezreel. This name comes unexpectedly
instead of 'Israel.' It seems to be used for two reasons, (i) to
shew that the name of Gomer's son in i. 4 has now lost its ominous
meaning, and that instead of 'scattering' His people, God will
bless them with a flesh 'sowing,' (ii) to introduce a final reference
to all three children. This last reference to Hosea's domestic
story is the more forcible when we place ii. 2-23 *after* iii., as
forming the conclusion of this part of the book.

23. This final verse not only gives a happier meaning to Jezreel;
it changes Lo-ruhamah to Ruhamah, and Lo-ammi to Ammi,
so that the children of the restored nation become 'pitied' and
'my people.'

iii. 1-5. See note on i. 10-ii. 1, for the theory that these verses
should come immediately after ii. 1, while ii. 2-23 turn from the
story of Gomer to that of Israel, and draw a promise of the nation's
progress towards restoration from that of the wife.

1. The prophet is encouraged by God to persist in his love of
his adulterous wife, even as He Himself still loves Israel. In spite
of being an adulteress, she still has in her husband a real **friend**.
But the **friend** may well be the paramour. In this case Hosea
and the **friend** correspond to Jehovah and **other gods**.

2 gods, and love cakes of raisins. So I bought her to me
   for fifteen *pieces* of silver, and an homer of barley, and an
3 half homer of barley : and I said unto her, Thou shalt abide
   for me many days ; thou shalt not play the harlot, and thou
   shalt not be any man's wife : so will I also be toward thee.
4 For the children of Israel shall abide many days without
   king, and without prince, and without sacrifice, and with-
5 out pillar, and without ephod or teraphim : afterward shall

---

love cakes of raisins. Though mentioned elsewhere as ordinary
food, they seem to have formed some part in the cult of heathen
deities, perhaps in honour of the gods whom they imagined to be
the givers of the grapes.

2. It is not obvious why Hosea had thus to buy his wife again.
If she had become another man's wife, the transaction would not
have been allowed. But it may have only been a private arrangement with the man whose mistress she had become. Or she may
well have fallen till she was reduced to the position of a slave-
concubine. In this case the 15 shekels represent half the ordinary
price of a slave (Exod. xxi. 32). If a homer and a half of barley
was worth another 15 shekels, the explanation would be complete.

and an half homer of barley. In any case the expression is
clumsily introduced. But the word for **half homer** is quite uncertain, and represents the Heb. 'lethech,' an unknown word
of which this is only the traditional meaning. The LXX reads
'a bottle of wine,' but this may simply be a guess. Another
explanation of the gifts in kind is that they were not paid, like
the shekels, to the man, but to Gomer herself, for her scanty
support until she is fully reinstated. A homer represented
10 ephahs.

3. A considerable period is to elapse, during which she is to
be wife to no man, not even to her true husband.

4-5. The personal story merges into the national one which it
illustrates. If the verses in ch. ii. be genuine, which promise
restoration, then *v.* 5 may stay. If the promises of restoration are
all later than Hosea, it must be omitted likewise.

4. without pillar. Such pillars were a relic of earlier
Canaanitish worship. They were afterwards condemned as
idolatrous (e.g. Deut. xii. 3), but they do not seem to have been
regarded as such in Hosea's time. These sacred stones were set up
in 'high places' as the accompaniment of **sacrifice**, and were
thought to represent the presence and power of the Deity. There
were ' pillars ' at Beth-el, Gibeon (2 Sam. xx. 8), etc.

without ephod or teraphim. The ephod is best explained,

the children of Israel return, and seek the LORD their God,
and David their king; and shall come with fear unto the
LORD and to his goodness in the latter days.

II. A SERIES OF PROPHECIES IN THE TIME OF INCREASING MORAL AND POLITICAL COLLAPSE. iv.–xiv. 9.

A. ISRAEL'S MORAL DECAY AND ITS SEQUEL. iv.–vii. 7.

I. JEHOVAH'S CONDEMNATION OF THE CORRUPTED NATION. iv.

iv. 1–4. *Moral corruption will bring inevitable distress on the land.*

Hear the word of the LORD, ye children of Israel: for **4**

---

not as the high priest's breastplate, but as an image of the deity
overlaid with gold-plating. In any case, its use was for ascertaining
the divine will (see e.g. 1 Sam. xxiii. 9 ff.). If it is to be connected
with the ephod worn by the priest, it may have been a kind of
apron, from the pockets of which the lots were drawn.

teraphim were images of ancestors, another relic of primitive
Semitic worship. Their human form is suggested by the story of
Michal putting one in David's bed and pretending that it was her
husband (1 Sam. xix. 13 ff.). For their use as oracles, see Ezek.
xxi. 21. Though Hosea does not condemn these adjuncts of worship,
he does not necessarily approve of them. It was at a later period,
owing to their abuse, that they were condemned and forbidden
(2 Kings xxiii. 24).

5. and David their king: i.e. a king who should be like the
greatest king of antiquity, whose name was so often connected
with a golden age of the future, which led to the expectation of
a Messiah who should be ' Son of David.' But it was in Judah,
not Israel, that David's dynasty continued, and this has caused
some to omit these words as a later Judaistic gloss. Those who
do not believe that Hosea's message contained a promise of
restoration, of course omit the whole verse.

shall come with fear. The bitter experience of the past shall
bring a new awe and reverence into their approach to Jehovah,
even though His **goodness** had been so amply shewn them.

iv.–xiv. 9. The rest of the book is much more difficult to divide
and summarise. Harper (*op. cit.*) traces as many as thirteen
prophecies, but there is no agreement as to topics and divisions.
The truth seems to be that Hosea utters a series of impassioned
and disjointed warnings and appeals in the name of his God,

the LORD hath a controversy with the inhabitants of the land, because there is no truth, nor mercy, nor knowledge
2 of God in the land. There is nought but swearing and breaking faith, and killing, and stealing, and committing

which were probably collected afterwards, but spoken as opportunity arose during a period of years. We may therefore imagine this part of his message as extending through the years which followed the death of the strong king, Jeroboam II, in 743 B.C. His able rule had held things together, but in the period of anarchy which followed the assassination of his son Zechariah, they went from bad to worse. There is no indication that Assyria had actually invaded Israel until after Hosea had spoken, so that the last prophecy must be dated before Tiglath-Pileser's invasion in 734 B.C.

Chapters iv.-x. seem to form a complete series, and the best division (though it is not strictly observed by the prophet) seems to be that of G. A. Smith (*op. cit.* p. 254), i.e. 'a people in decay morally' (iv.-vii. 7), and 'a people in decay politically' (vii. 8-x.).

Another difficulty of the book, as soon as we leave the first three chapters, is the obviously corrupt condition of the text. Some editors have made wholesale emendations and excisions. These are not followed in these notes except in cases where nothing can be done with the present text. (See Introd. pp. 19, 20.)

Ch. iv. opens the subject by a general condemnation of the corrupted nation. It is succeeded by three other sections of iv.-vii. 7, dealing more specifically with the same theme of moral decay, viz. v. 1–14, Jehovah's condemnation of the priests and princes; v. 15–vii. 2, Jehovah will not spare unless repentance is real; and vii. 3–7, Their kings are involved in the general degradation.

iv. 1-4. Moral taint brings a curse on the soil and the population, and man involves all animate creation with him in his fall (cf. Rom. viii. 22).

1. the Lord hath a controversy. Hosea's image of Jehovah as accusing His people in a court of law is repeated and elaborated by many other prophets (e.g. Is. i.).

no truth, nor mercy: i.e. fidelity and brotherly love, as may be gathered from their opposites in *v.* 2.

nor knowledge of God: i.e. knowledge which arouses conscience. 'It is knowledge that is followed by shame, or by love, or by reverence, or by the sense of a duty.' (G. A. Smith, *op. cit.* p. 322. His whole chapter on the subject is worth reading.)

adultery; they break out, and blood toucheth blood.
Therefore shall the land mourn, and every one that dwel- 3
leth therein shall languish, with the beasts of the field and
the fowls of heaven; yea, the fishes of the sea also shall
be taken away. Yet let no man strive, neither let any man 4
reprove; for thy people are as they that strive with the
priest.

5-11. *Israel's religious leaders are the chief cause of moral collapse.*

And thou shalt stumble in the day, and the prophet also 5
shall stumble with thee in the night; and I will destroy
thy mother. My people are destroyed for lack of know- 6

---

2. blood toucheth blood: i.e. one murder follows upon another.
The assassination of Zechariah probably caused an outbreak of
deeds of violence.

3. Therefore shall the land mourn: or 'is mourning,' suggesting that a drought is already present, and nature has begun
to reflect man's condition.

the fishes of the sea: probably in the lakes, which would be
dried up.

4. Yet let no man strive, etc.: i.e. the blame lay, not with
ordinary men, but with their religious leaders.

as they that strive with the priest. These words as they
stand suggest that to contradict a priest is a heinous offence. But,
unless they are bitterly sarcastic, they can scarcely mean this in
the light of the condemnation of the priest which follows. Again,
it is not stated who 'thou' is meant for in *v.* 5, although the
natural word to supply is 'priest,' as coupled with the word
'prophet' which follows. Following a clue given by LXX **strive**
has been emended to a word for 'priests,' which is used (e.g. in
x. 5) for the Baal priests. So most editors alter the text thus:
'Thy people is like their priestlings.' The other word for priest
at the end of the verse can now be given to *v.* 5, as a vocative,
i.e. 'Thou, O priest, shalt stumble.'

5. And thou: for the text, see foregoing note.

in the night: a natural sequel to **in the day,** as the prophets
follow the priests in the misuse of their office.

thy mother. In the light of what follows, it seems better to
take this of the whole Israelite stock than of the priestly caste.

6. The rejection of the priests of the northern kingdom is
not because they began by being schismatic, but because they

ledge: because thou hast rejected knowledge, I will also
reject thee, that thou shalt be no priest to me: seeing thou
hast forgotten the law of thy God, I also will forget thy
7 children. As they were multiplied, so they sinned against
8 me: I will change their glory into shame. They feed on
the sin of my people, and set their heart on their iniquity.
9 And it shall be, like people, like priest: and I will punish
10 them for their ways, and will reward them their doings. And
they shall eat, and not have enough; they shall commit

---

ended by being unpriestly, cf. Mal. ii. 7. 'The priest's lips should
keep knowledge.'

the law of thy God: i.e. the *Torah*, which included oral
instruction as well as any laws which had found their way into
writing. For the **law** current in Hosea's time, see Introd. p. 16.

thy children. This implies an ending of the line of priests,
for the office descended from father to son. Possibly the threat
against 'thy mother' at the end of *v.* 5, and 'thy children' at the
end of *v.* 6, is reminiscent of Hosea's domestic story in chs. i.–iii.

7. As they were multiplied. Doubtless the priesthood was
increased by the prosperity of Jeroboam's reign, and attracted
unworthy men into it.

I will change their glory. Following the Syriac version, an
emendation has been made to 'they have changed.' **Their glory** is
that of the priest's office, which was evidently held in high honour.

8. They feed on the sin of my people. The priests received
payment when the people made a sin-offering (2 Kings xii. 16).
Therefore the more the people sinned, the more lucrative these
degenerate priests found it. But if this custom was only of a later
date than Hosea, the words must mean that they increased their
gain by 'encouraging the people in a false conception of Jehovah.'
(Harper, *op. cit.* p. 287.)

9. And it shall be, like people, like priest: or rather ' it *is*,'
for the priests have reduced themselves to the spiritual level of
the people, and so shall be punished for ignoring the high
privileges of their office.

10. And they shall eat, etc. The subject seems still to be the
priests, not the people, who will not get satisfaction from the
sacrificial feasts.

they shall commit whoredom. The appalling immorality
which the Canaanite religions had introduced in Israel consisted
in sinful practices between the priests and the women who came
to the Sanctuaries. This was supposed to please the gods of the
land who presided over the productive powers of nature.

whoredom, and shall not increase: because they have left off to take heed to the LORD. Whoredom and wine and 11 new wine take away the understanding.

12–14. *Immoral worship makes the whole nation immoral.*

My people ask counsel at their stock, and their staff de- 12 clareth unto them: for the spirit of whoredom hath caused them to err, and they have gone a whoring from under their God. They sacrifice upon the tops of the mountains, 13 and burn incense upon the hills, under oaks and poplars and terebinths, because the shadow thereof is good: therefore your daughters commit whoredom, and your brides

---

11. It is a tempting emendation to place this verse after the first half of *v.* 12. In that case it refers to a new topic, and is a general truth which Hosea proceeds to apply, not to the priests, but to the people. If no change is made in the order, it must still refer to the priests, adding drunkenness to their other sins.

12. ask counsel at their stock : i.e. at the wood of the teraphim, which the priests encourage, instead of higher means of spiritual counsel. But it may be a case of parallelism, **stock** and **staff** referring to the same thing.

their staff declareth unto them: probably some form of diviner's wand, another heathenish way of seeking God through the priests. But the whole verse may refer to survivals of primitive tree-worship (W. Robertson Smith, *Religion of the Semites,* p. 196).

the spirit of whoredom. The immoral worship of the sanctuaries in the name of religion was bound to loosen the morals of the whole community. The rest of the verse points to Jehovah as Israel's true husband, and suggests the lesson which Hosea had already taught through his unfaithful wife. The two things, literal whoredom and metaphorical, are often combined in the prophetic writings. And it is an abiding truth that the debasing of religious ideals leads to the decay of national morals.

13. the tops of the mountains...under oaks, etc. The localities in which nature-worshippers specially looked for the divine presence were bare hill-tops and the shade of trees. A frequent phrase is 'every high hill and every green tree' (e.g. 2 Kings xvii. 10 and Jer. ii. 20).

therefore your daughters, etc. Immorality in every day life

14 commit adultery. I will not punish your daughters when they commit whoredom, nor your brides when they commit adultery; for they themselves go apart with whores, and they sacrifice with the harlots: and the people that doth not understand shall be overthrown.

15. Judah is warned against inviting similar punishment.

15 Though thou, Israel, play the harlot, yet let not Judah offend; and come not ye unto Gilgal, neither go ye up to Beth-aven, nor swear, As the LORD liveth.

16-19. Such obstinacy will only bring shame.

16 For Israel hath behaved himself stubbornly, like a stubborn

---

is the natural result. But it began under the sanctions of religion. For **brides**, read as R.V. mg. 'daughters in law.'

14. The real responsibility lies, not with the women, who have been affected by the nation's tendency, but with the men, and especially the priests, who have **themselves** practised the evil. In the licentious worship of Ashtaroth, and of the Asherah, the devotees were actually regarded as 'holy.' 'It is vain for the men of a nation to practise impurity, and fancy that nevertheless they can keep their womenkind chaste' (G. A. Smith, *op. cit.* p. 259).

15. This verse may be a later Judaistic insertion, its language being suggested by the warnings (to Israel) of Amos v. 5, 'Seek not Beth-el, nor enter into Gilgal, and pass not to Beer-sheba.' It this be the case, since **Beth-aven**, 'house of vanity,' is a contemptuous name for Beth-el, 'house of God,' it has been suggested that a third place-name has dropped out of the text; **nor swear** at Beer-sheba ('the well of the oath'). But, in favour of the genuineness of the verse, it is to be noted that these sanctuaries were easily accessible for the people of the southern kingdom.

Gilgal was an ancient sanctuary, but its corruption was a by-word, cf. ix. 15. Its site has been identified, close to Jericho. **Beth-aven** is mentioned again in x. 5 as the centre of calf-worship.

nor swear, As the Lord liveth. This was not sinful in itself, but only when combined with a corrupted worship, in which Jehovah was confused with local deities. But if the words 'at Beer-sheba' are to be inserted, as suggested above, Amos throws further light on the passage by his denunciation of those who say, 'As thy God, O Dan, liveth'; and say, 'As the way (or manner) of Beer-sheba liveth' (Amos viii. 14). It was the way the swearing was done at that sanctuary which made it blasphemous.

16. As the verse stands, it suggests the idea of a lamb wandering

heifer: now will the LORD feed them as a lamb in a large
place. Ephraim is joined to idols; let him alone. Their 17, 18
drink is become sour: they commit whoredom continually;
her rulers dearly love shame. The wind hath wrapped her 19
up in its wings; and they shall be ashamed because of
their sacrifices.

2. JEHOVAH'S CONDEMNATION OF THE PRIESTS
AND PRINCES. v. 1–14.

v. 1–7. *A message to those who rule.*

Hear this, O ye priests, and hearken, ye house of Israel, 5

---

unprotected, and a prey to wild beasts. But this is not the way
the simile is used elsewhere (e.g. Is. xxx. 23 and frequently in
the Psalms). It seems better therefore to take the second half of
the verse either (1) as a question: 'Can Jehovah now feed them?'
or (2) as an exclamation: 'Now would Jehovah feed them!' but
their obstinacy prevents Him. The thought is that as the nation
has behaved like a stubborn heifer, it is impossible for God to
shepherd it gently, as a lamb.

17. The central and dominant tribe is here named for the whole
kingdom. This use of **Ephraim** is frequent in the rest of the book,
e.g. v. 3.

let him alone. As the nation is wedded to a corrupted Jehovah
worship which centres in idols, it must be left to its fate.

18. The text of this verse is hopelessly corrupt. The versions
give diverse renderings, and many emendations have been suggested by critics. The first clause is best taken as in R.V. marg.
'Their carouse is over' (following the Vulgate '*separatum est con-
vivium eorum*'), i.e. when their drunken carouse is over, they are
wont to make fornication its sequel. Some render 'A band of
topers! They devote themselves to harlotry.' Perhaps the last
clause is 'Her rulers love shame rather than her pride' (following LXX), i.e. 'they prefer base things to Jehovah.' Or
(based on the Masoretic Text), 'the princes love (to say) give ye,
and this is a shame,' i.e. they ask for bribes, and so turn justice
into shame.

19. The wind hath wrapped her up, etc.: i.e. she is certain to
be caught in a whirlwind of Assyrian attack.

v. 1. In this section Hosea extends his terrible message to
temporal as well as spiritual rulers, and through them to the
people for whom they are responsible. The opening sentence
marks this threefold address.

and give ear, O house of the king, for unto you pertaineth
the judgement; for ye have been a snare at Mizpah, and
2 a net spread upon Tabor. And the revolters are gone deep
3 in making slaughter; but I am a rebuker of them all. I
know Ephraim, and Israel is not hid from me: for now, O
Ephraim, thou hast committed whoredom, Israel is defiled.
4 Their doings will not suffer them to turn unto their God:
for the spirit of whoredom is within them, and they know
5 not the LORD. And the pride of Israel doth testify to his
face: therefore Israel and Ephraim shall stumble in their

---

house of the king : i.e. the court. Perhaps the words were
spoken while Zechariah, the feeble son of Jeroboam, was still on
the throne. Harper suggests the reign of Menahem, when the
judgement began to fall in the shape of trouble from Assyria
(2 Kings xv. 18-20).

unto you pertaineth the judgement. These words mean more
than that the rulers ought to be giving judgement, and seem to
refer to Jehovah's judgement on them all. So R.V. mg. 'against
you is the judgement.' Perhaps the ambiguity was intentional.

at Mizpah, and...upon Tabor: hill sanctuaries, one in Gilead,
and sacred since the story of Jacob (Gen. xxxi. 45-54), and the
other farther north, above the plain of Jezreel.

2. And the revolters are gone deep in making slaughter. It
is difficult to see the connexion of these words as they stand.
The variations of the versions suggest a corrupt text. The generally accepted emendation alters to 'A pit they have made deep
upon Shittim.' This gives three parallel clauses (akin to the
threefold address which precedes in *v.* 1), each giving a different
means of catching birds or animals, i.e. by 'snare,' 'net,' and
'pit,' and connecting this laying of traps with *three* localities.
Shittim was where the people gave themselves to worship the
god Baal-peor, as they encamped at the place of that name on
the way from Egypt (Numb. xxv. 1-3).

3. It is impossible to deceive God by retaining the appearance
of being His worshippers.

4. the spirit of whoredom : see note on iv. 12. It dulled
their apprehension of the divine nature, and led to the state
already described in iv. 1 (see note).

5. the pride of Israel: either (1) the people's false pride,
which witnesses against them, or (2) the glory of Israel (as
R.V. mg. 'excellency'), meaning Jehovah. The former meaning
accords better with the sense required, and follows the LXX.
The words occur again in vii. 10.

iniquity; Judah also shall stumble with them. They shall 6
go with their flocks and with their herds to seek the LORD;
but they shall not find him: he hath withdrawn himself
from them. They have dealt treacherously against the 7
LORD; for they have borne strange children: now shall
the new moon devour them with their fields.

*8-14. Punishment will fall on both Israel and Judah,
from which no appeal to Assyria can bring escape.*

Blow ye the cornet in Gibeah, and the trumpet in Ramah: 8
sound an alarm at Beth-aven; behind thee, O Benjamin.
Ephraim shall become a desolation in the day of rebuke: 9

6. This verse shews that their corrupted worship with its
abundant sacrifices was still nominally offered to Jehovah, but
was not acceptable to Him.

7. Hosea reverts to the metaphor of unfaithful wife and
bastard children so familiar from chs. i.–iii.

now shall the new moon devour them. Possibly this refers to
the corrupted worship of the festival with which their lunar month
began. But **new moon** may stand for 'month,' signifying that
'within a month ruin may overtake them' (Harper, *op. cit.* p. 271).

8-9. The prophet now foresees the invasion by their Assyrian
enemies. There is a sudden rousing of the clans to battle, but
the result is utter defeat.

8. Gibeah...Ramah...Beth-aven (i.e. Beth-el). These may
represent elevated spots from which the signals to assemble were
made. Or they may mark the Assyrian line of advance. The
curious thing is that they are so far south, and partly correspond
to the Assyrian advance on Jerusalem in 701 B.C. in Is. xxx.
28–34, where not a call to arms meets them, but universal panic,
and yet they fail to take the holy city. ('Ramah trembleth;
Gibeah of Saul is fled.')

behind thee, O Benjamin. These words have been explained
as the ancient warcry of the Benjamites (see Judges v. 14, 'after
thee, Benjamin'); or a warning that, after the fall of Ephraim,
'the enemy is after thee, O Benjamin.' The LXX 'Benjamin is
amazed' has suggested the rendering 'make Benjamin to tremble.'
It is to be noted that in this whole passage (*vv.* 5-14) the mention
of the southern kingdom is so interwoven with the message, that
the modern critical effort to remove all references to Judah as later
additions is more strained than usual. Harper would simply
substitute 'Israel' for 'Judah' thoughout.

9. When the crisis comes, the desolation of the land is foretold
as the certain sequel.

among the tribes of Israel have I made known that which
10 shall surely be. The princes of Judah are like them that
remove the landmark: I will pour out my wrath upon them
11 like water. Ephraim is oppressed, he is crushed in judgement; because he was content to walk after the command.
12 Therefore am I unto Ephraim as a moth, and to the house
13 of Judah as rottenness. When Ephraim saw his sickness,
and Judah *saw* his wound, then went Ephraim to Assyria,
and sent to king Jareb: but he is not able to heal you,

---

10. that remove the landmark : a particularly mean form of
theft, suggesting how degraded the princes were. The curse on
those who remove their neighbour's landmark (Deut. xxvii. 17)
is made familiar in the Church of England by the Commination
Service.

11. The Heb. gives a passive sense to **crushed** and **oppressed**,
implying that this is God's judgement upon them. But those who
follow the LXX make the participles active, rendering 'Ephraim
practises oppression, he breaks down right,' his action being
explained by the clause that follows. In the light of the following
note, the latter sense is to be preferred.

content to walk after the command. If these are the words
they must be put in the form of a question. But it seems best
(see R.V. mg. following the versions) to read 'vanity' instead of
the command, meaning idolatry.

12. a moth...rottenness. As the moth secretly devours a gar-
ment, and dry rot slowly and inwardly devours wood-work, so
the mills of God will slowly grind the nation in punishment.
Begin the verse as R.V. mg. 'And I was.'

13. When the state was thus inwardly corrupt, it was useless
to appeal to Assyria for help against the wound caused by
Jehovah. For the metaphor, cf. vi. 1.

Judah *saw* **his wound.** Hosea does not state that Judah appealed to Assyria. That was the policy which commended itself
to king Ahaz, when Israel and Syria invaded Judah in 734 B.C.
(2 Kings xvi. 7). There can be an allusion to this only if we suppose the words were added later. But Uzziah was dead, and Judah,
like Israel, was subject to new internal difficulties, and we can
imagine that there was already a pro-Assyrian party in Judah.

sent to king Jareb. The name is quite unknown. Of the
many explanations offered, the best seems to be that it is a nick-
name, 'King Combative,' probably referring to Tiglath-Pileser.
It occurs again in x. 6.

not able to heal you. On the contrary, the policy of Menahem
proved to be the beginning of the end for Israel.

neither shall he cure you of your wound. For I will be unto 14
Ephraim as a lion, and as a young lion to the house of
Judah: I, even I, will tear and go away; I will carry off,
and there shall be none to deliver.

3. JEHOVAH WILL NOT SPARE UNLESS REPENTANCE IS REAL. v. 15-vii. 2.

15. *Jehovah waits for them to repent.*

I will go and return to my place, till they acknowledge 15
their offence, and seek my face: in their affliction they will
seek me earnestly.

vi. 1-6. *A superficial repentance is useless.*

Come, and let us return unto the LORD: for he hath torn, **6**
and he will heal us; he hath smitten, and he will bind us
up. After two days will he revive us: on the third day he 2
will raise us up, and we shall live before him. And let us 3

---

14. Divine retribution for national corruption could not be
avoided by foreign alliances.

15. This verse is best regarded as introducing a new prophecy
dealing with repentance. The thought in it is entirely alien to
what precedes. God is represented as waiting until repentance
comes as the result of affliction. But the verses that follow reveal
the possibility of a confession which is only on the surface, and
therefore cannot be accepted.

vi. 1-3. At first sight these words, put into the mouth of the
nation, appear to be a real act of repentance, and certainly they
are full of beauty. But the sequel shews that their beauty is no
more than verbal, and they really represent a merely external
repentance, which almost blasphemously takes it for granted that
their utterance is absolutely certain to bring forgiveness without
more ado.

1. The pathetic thing is that Jehovah is waiting for Israel to
return, and when they do, it is not in such a way, or with such a
conception of Him, that He can heal them.

for he hath torn: as the 'lion' had done in v. 14.

2. After two days...on the third day: This is only a
poetical way of saying 'in two or three days,' i.e. at once. To
see a reference to the Resurrection, as Pusey did, is not in keeping with more modern forms of interpretation of the prophets.

3. They make the right resolve, but the weak and easily
satisfied deity whom they picture is not the real Jehovah.

know, let us follow on to know the LORD; his going forth
is sure as the morning: and he shall come unto us as the
rain, as the latter rain that watereth the earth.

4 O Ephraim, what shall I do unto thee? O Judah, what shall
I do unto thee? for your goodness is as a morning cloud, and
5 as the dew that goeth early away. Therefore have I hewed
them by the prophets; I have slain them by the words of my
mouth: and thy judgements are *as* the light that goeth
6 forth. For I desire mercy, and not sacrifice; and the
knowledge of God more than burnt offerings.

---

his going forth is sure as the morning : i.e. his response is
as sure as that day follows night. But the LXX reading suggests
the rendering 'when we seek him, then we shall find him,' a
simple and easy process.

the rain...the latter rain. The first is the heavy rain of
winter, and the second the rain of spring, which was also needed
for the ripening of the crops.

4. Jehovah now speaks, in despair rather than in anger. For
He knows how transient their words of repentance are, like the
early clouds which are soon dried up by the sun.

5. hewed them by the prophets : i.e. pronounced sentence
of death by the mouth of the prophets. It is generally taken to
refer to the prophets of the past, but it suits better to consider it
as a prophetic perfect, describing the present result of their sham
repentance.

and thy judgements, etc. Much better sense is obtained by
reading 'my,' as in R.V. mg. But a combination of the R.V.
text and mg. gives 'and my judgement is like the light that goeth
forth,' i.e. either (1) the light of the rising sun that all can see, or
(2) the lightning with its sudden flash.

6. What the people have failed to realise is that knowledge of
Jehovah involves 'leal love' (G. A. Smith) both of Himself and
of their fellows. The prophets are so full of warnings against
mere outwardness in religious observances, that some have been
led to think that they condemn all sacrifices. But surely it is
only the letter without the spirit that they treat with scorn (see
Introd. p. 14). This verse is famous as having been quoted by
our Lord on two occasions. In both cases there is no condemnation of outward acts of religion in 'I desire mercy, and not
sacrifice.' The words were spoken as a protest against those who
complained that He ate with publicans and sinners (S. Matth. ix.
13), and later, when the Pharisees insisted on a mechanical

7–vii. 2. Their defilement is too deep-seated to make
pardon possible.

But they like Adam have transgressed the covenant: there 7
have they dealt treacherously against me. Gilead is a city 8
of them that work iniquity, it is stained with blood. And 9
as troops of robbers wait for a man, so the company of
priests murder in the way toward Shechem: yea, they have
committed lewdness. In the house of Israel I have seen 10
an horrible thing: there whoredom is *found* in Ephraim,
Israel is defiled. Also, O Judah, there is an harvest ap- 11

---

observance of the Sabbath (S. Matth. xii. 7). It will be noticed
that the 'mercy' (love, or kindness) is to be shewn in relation to
men, as a result of a right relation to God.

The words express a general truth, already expressed by Amos
(v. 21–24) 'Though ye offer me your burnt offerings and meal
offerings, I will not accept them....But let judgement roll down
as wáters,' and also familiar in Ps. li. 'Thou desirest truth in the
inward parts...thou delightest not in sacrifice,' and in Samuel's
rebuke to Saul when he pleaded that he had kept the 'devoted'
things in order to sacrifice them, 'Behold, to obey is better than
sacrifice' (1 Sam. xv. 22).

7. But they like Adam have transgressed the covenant. The
translation is quite uncertain. If the R.V. is right, the reference
must be to Adam's act of disobedience. Two other renderings
must be mentioned, (1) 'like men,' a more likely translation of
the Hebrew (as given in A.V.), and meaning 'like ordinary men,'
without Israel's privileges (but this is a forced explanation), (2) 'in
Adam,' the name of a place (as in Josh. iii. 16) or 'in Admah.'
A place-name is certainly required to explain the word 'there'
in what follows (unless, as G. A. Smith, 'there' refers to Gilead
and Shechem in the next verse; this, however, is improbable).

8. Gilead is a city: But Gilead was a district, not a city.
Perhaps it refers to Mizpah, its capital (see v. 1). Its uncivilised
mountaineers might well cause it to be 'tracked with bloody
foot-prints.'

9. The priests themselves were no better than bandits on the
road to the sanctuary of Shechem. The word for **'lewdness'**
need not mean more than general 'villainy.'

10. whoredom. It is uncertain whether the sense is literal
or spiritual. But one involved the other, for idolatry encouraged
immorality.

11. Judah is to expect a harvest of punishment for similar sins.
But if the **harvest** is in a bad sense, how can it be when the

pointed for thee, when I bring again the captivity of my
people.

7   When I would heal Israel, then is the iniquity of Ephraim
discovered, and the wickedness of Samaria; for they commit falsehood: and the thief entereth in, *and* the troop of
2 robbers spoileth without. And they consider not in their
hearts that I remember all their wickedness: now have
their own doings beset them about; they are before my face.

4. THEIR KINGS ARE INVOLVED IN THE GENERAL DEGRADATION. vii. 3–7.

3 They make the king glad with their wickedness, and the
4 princes with their lies. They are all adulterers; they are

---

captivity is over? It is not easy to find an answer. But it seems
better to end the sense with the first half of the verse, and join the
rest with vii. 1, reading, 'when I would bring again the captivity
of my people, when I would heal Israel.'

If **bring again the captivity of** must imply that the exile has
already taken place, then the verse must be post-exilic, and may
be compared with Amos ix. 14, as a later addition to the book.
But the phrase need mean no more than 'restore to prosperity,'
without any actual captivity, as in Ezek. xvi. 53; Job xlii. 10.

vii. 1. See foregoing note. God's readiness to forgive only
discloses the extent of the corruption. Instances are given in
housebreaking at home, and highway robbery abroad.

2. They persuaded themselves that all will be forgotten and
forgiven, and so they become entangled in their own evil practices,
which witness against them.

3–7. The uncertain text of this section makes a difficult
passage yet more obscure. But the general sense is plain.
Hitherto the prophet's universal condemnation has stopped short
of the throne. Now, as the climax of their corruption, he ven-
tures to denounce the monarchy of his day, as decadent,
debauched, and unstable. The court is full of immorality and
drunkenness, and these things lead to outbreaks of passion, the
final result being that one king after another falls by the hand of
a usurper.

3. The collapse of true kingship came with Jeroboam's death.
His successors, beginning with Zechariah, were infected by the
baseness and the treachery around them.

They make the king glad. A trifling alteration gives 'they
anoint,' but the change is scarcely needed.

4. Their lust is like a baker's oven, which can be left alone

as an oven heated by the baker; he ceaseth to stir *the fire*,
from the kneading of the dough until it be leavened.. On 5
the day of our king the princes made themselves sick with
the heat of wine; he stretched out his hand with scorners.
For they have made ready their heart like an oven, whiles 6
they lie in wait: their baker sleepeth all the night; in the
morning it burneth as a flaming fire. They are all hot as 7
an oven, and devour their judges; all their kings are fallen:
there is none among them that calleth unto me.

B. ISRAEL'S POLITICAL DECAY AND ITS SEQUEL.

vii. 8–x. 15.

1. ISRAEL'S FOOLISH FOREIGN POLICY. vii. 8–viii. 3.

8–12. *Their weak and hesitating attitude towards
Egypt and Assyria.*

Ephraim, he mixeth himself among the peoples; Ephraim 8

---

when the fire is well blazing, and trusted to heat up again when
the dough is fermented. Even so their lust when gratified will
go on burning till it is stirred again. Hosea enlarges on this
simile in *vv.* 6 and 7. This is one of many explanations, but it
seems the simplest. For another metaphor from the oven, see vii. 8.

5. This verse suggests a carouse on the king's birthday, which
results in an act of violence. Perhaps it is the usurper who
'stretched out his hand.'

6. A few hours of the night pass, while the conspirators nurse
their plot, which is carried out in the morning. **Their baker** can
easily be emended to 'their anger,' but *v.* 4 makes the meaning
plain enough without doing so.

7. In the heat of their passion they destroy their rulers (**judges**
=rulers), so that one king after another is assassinated, and yet
no one thinks of appealing to their heavenly King, in spite of the
increasing anarchy that results.

all their kings. Shallum murdered Zechariah, and was in
turn assassinated by Menahem, in whose reign these words were
probably spoken. But the anarchy continued. The next king
Pekahiah fell before his captain Pekah, and Pekah before Hoshea.
All this took place in little more than a dozen years, and was in
keeping with earlier usurpations in the unhappy northern kingdom, such as those of Zimri, Omri, and Jehu (see 2 Kings xv.
8–30, and Introd. p. 3).

8 ff. No clear division is to be found, but this is the point at

9 is a cake not turned. Strangers have devoured his strength,
and he knoweth *it* not : yea, gray hairs are here and there
10 upon him, and he knoweth *it* not. And the pride of Israel
doth testify to his face : yet they have not returned unto

---

which the *moral* element in Israel's decay, which has been
uppermost in the section iv.–vii. 7, is more in the background,
and the *political* element, which has not yet received much stress,
is the chief theme of the prophet until the end of ch. x. Again it
is possible to subdivide this part of the book into four sections,
beginning at vii. 8 ; viii. 4 ; x. 1 ; and x. 11.

8. This verse summarises in two epigrams the weakness of
the foreign and of the domestic policy of Israel. (1) In his
relations with other nations, it is not merely that he engages
in commercial and other relations, which might be wise and
profitable, but **he mixeth himself**, i.e. he 'pours himself
out,' and loses his distinctiveness by merging his way of life with
theirs. The prophets persistently recommended a policy of
isolation, and it was due to its observance by Judah that
Jerusalem stood so long without becoming the vassal city of
foreign powers. It was not so easy for the northern kingdom,
from its geographical position, to pursue a similar policy, but it
was by spontaneous and mistaken efforts in the opposite direction
that Samaria brought its own ruin.

(2) The other epigram describes a home policy which could
be traced in many directions. The nation only half developed its
life, with glaring contrasts as a result ; it was as **a cake not
turned**. A common article of food in the East is a flat round
cake, which has to be turned over and cooked on both sides to
make it eatable ; otherwise it is burnt up on one side and raw on
the other. G. A. Smith (whose exposition of the whole passage
is well worth reading, *op. cit.* pp. 270–276) instances such contrasts, for Israel or for any nation, as the existence of the very
rich and the very poor side by side (the condition revealed by
Amos), outward religiosity and inward wickedness, varying
foreign alliances, first hot and then cold, and lack of thoroughness
in the national character. 'How better describe a half-fed
people, a half-cultured society, a half-lived religion, a half-
hearted policy, than by a half-baked scone?'

9. The rest of this section elaborates the epigrams of *v.* 8
dealing first with the 'mixing.' Their boasted commercial relations have only resulted in their own life and character being
sapped by other nations, and then in the unperceived advance of
senile decay.

10. the pride of Israel. See note on v. 5. The probable
meaning is that their own arrogance testifies against them, and

the LORD their God, nor sought him, for all this. And 11
Ephraim is like a silly dove, without understanding : they
call unto Egypt, they go to Assyria. When they shall go, 12
I will spread my net upon them; I will bring them down
as the fowls of the heaven: I will chastise them, as their
congregation hath heard.

13-16. *They only reveal thereby their unfaithfulness to
their covenant with Jehovah.*

Woe unto them! for they have wandered from me; des- 13
truction unto them! for they have trespassed against me:
though I would redeem them, yet they have spoken lies
against me. And they have not cried unto me with their 14
heart, but they howl upon their beds: they assemble them-

---

they fail to see this and repent of it. G. A. Smith interprets it as
the proper pride of the nation, outraged by humiliating alliances
(*op. cit.* p. 275).

11-12. A new and telling simile. Their vacillating policy, in
appealing first to Egypt and then to Assyria, is compared to the
action of **a silly dove**, which flutters hither and thither (perhaps
responding to first one mate and then another), and all the while
fails to notice the bird-net which is about to catch it. It is Jehovah who has spread the net of punishment, but they are too
engrossed with their negotiations to notice it.

For the policy of alliances, first with Egypt and then with
Assyria, cf. xii. 1, and see also 2 Kings xv. 19 and xvii. 4. It
was this policy which nearly brought the ruin of Judah likewise,
in the reign of Ahaz (2 Kings xvi. 7 and Is. xxx. 1, 2).

12. as their congregation hath heard. The sense is feeble,
and the text probably corrupt. Certainly the people had not been
left by Amos and Hosea without public warning.

13-16. Israel is pictured as claiming justification for turning
to other saviours. They say that they have done their best to
satisfy Jehovah's demands, and He has not helped them in return.
But really they had quite failed to give Him what was demanded
of them, and their frantic entreaties were only for the sake of
worldly advantage.

13. spoken lies against me : by misrepresenting His true
character.

14. upon their beds : or better, 'beside their altars,' by a
slight emendation.

they assemble themselves : i.e. for worship. But if the R.V. mg.

15 selves for corn and wine, they rebel against me. Though
   I have taught and strengthened their arms, yet do they
16 imagine mischief against me. They return, but not to *him
   that is* on high; they are like a deceitful bow: their princes
   shall fall by the sword for the rage of their tongue: this
   shall be their derision in the land of Egypt.

   viii. 1–3. *It is therefore useless to appeal to Him when
   invasion befalls them.*

8 *Set* the trumpet to thy mouth. As an eagle *he cometh*
   against the house of the LORD: because they have transgressed my covenant, and trespassed against my law.
2 They shall cry unto me, My God, we Israel know thee.

---

is right, 'they cut themselves,' it suggests a frenzied worship like
that of the devotees of Baal who 'cut themselves...with knives'
(1 Kings xviii. 28).

15. Their attitude to Jehovah shewed base ingratitude for what
He had done for them.

16. not to *him that is* on high: i.e. not to their heavenly
Saviour, but to earthly ones. But the Heb. can scarcely mean
this. Harper suggests emending to 'they return to Baal,' and
takes the previous verses as describing idolatrous worship (*op.
cit.* p. 307), but this does not fit so well with the earlier part of
the verse.

like a deceitful bow: or 'a bow that swerves,' i.e. one that
cannot be trusted, but shoots in the wrong direction (cf. Ps. lxxviii.
57 and cxx. 2).

for the rage of their tongue. The heads of the party which
turned to Egypt may have shewn special insolence. Now the
result will only be a collapse at which Egypt itself will laugh.

viii. 1–3. This forms a sequel to the foregoing section. The
only thing left is to sound the alarm, for the Assyrian is at hand,
and will soon be in pursuit. This is the inevitable result of
breaking their covenant with Jehovah, although they protest to
the end that their relation with Him is satisfactory.

1. *Set* **the trumpet**: God's command to Hosea.

As an eagle: the foe approaches with the strength and swift-
ness of an eagle.

the house of the Lord: generally explained as 'the land of
Israel,' but the phrase is unusual.

against my law. It does not seem necessary to regard the
words as a later addition, for a *Torah* was already in existence.

2. My God, we Israel know thee. This is their final cry, when

Israel hath cast off that which is good: the enemy shall 3
pursue him.

2. THE FUTILITY OF SETTING UP KINGS AND MAKING
GODS. viii. 4–ix. 17.

*4–8. Because of their kings and idols they will reap
the whirlwind.*

They have set up kings, but not by me; they have made 4
princes, and I knew it not: of their silver and their gold
have they made them idols, that they may be cut off. He 5
hath cast off thy calf, O Samaria; mine anger is kindled

---

their fate is at length perceived. The pronouns combine a personal with a national appeal. The appeal was useless, because
not accompanied by any seeking of **that which is good**.

4. The section of the book which begins here is concerned with
two kindred evils, the national trust in a series of man-made
kings, such as could not possibly be the Lord's anointed, and also
in a series of man-made gods, the making of which was sure to
rouse the righteous wrath of Jehovah. As the larger division beginning at vii. 8 opened with a double epigram, such is the case
with *v.* 4. G. A. Smith calls it 'artificial kings and artificial
gods,' the link between them being that they are both the work
of men's hands. He notes that 'till near the close of his book the
idols of the sanctuary and the puppets of the throne form the twin
targets of his scorn' *(op. cit. p. 277).*

but not by me: either (1) because they were so many of them
regicides, who reached the throne by foul means, or (2) because
from the outset the northern kingdom was schismatical. If the
latter is the right explanation, as most commentators think, it
shews that Hosea's judgement was adverse to the division of the
kingdom, an attitude different from the prophets of the period,
and from the author of Kings (see 1 Kings xi. 29, 31). See
Introd. p. 17, and note on i. 4.

that they may be cut off: i.e., not the people, but the idols,
or the silver and gold.

5. He hath cast off thy calf, O Samaria. The plain reference
is to the golden calves set up by Jeroboam in Dan and Beth-el.
Possibly these would-be symbols of Jehovah were also to be found
in Samaria (cf. *v.* 6), but the capital may be used as 'Ephraim'
so frequently is, a part standing for the whole country. Another
rendering is 'Thy calf is loathsome.'

against them : how long will it be ere they attain to inno-
6 cency? For from Israel is even this ; the workman made
   it, and it is no God : yea, the calf of Samaria shall be
7 broken in pieces. For they sow the wind, and they shall
   reap the whirlwind : he hath no standing corn ; the blade
   shall yield no meal ; if so be it yield, strangers shall swal-
8 low it up. Israel is swallowed up : now are they among
   the nations as a vessel wherein is no pleasure.

> 9–14. *They have invited Jehovah's rejection by their*
> *trust in foreign powers, in altars and sacrifices,*
> *and in their own strongholds.*

9 For they are gone up to Assyria, *like* a wild ass alone by
10 himself: Ephraim hath hired lovers. Yea, though they

---

innocency. The word may mean 'freedom from punishment,'
which follows naturally on the preceding words. Or it may be a
pious gloss. But it makes quite good sense in its ordinary meaning.

6. from Israel is even this: i.e. **this** is merely a man-made
idol. 'Instead of Israel being from God, the god is from Israel,'
Horton, *Minor Prophets*, 1. p. 46.

7. The results of Israel's policy are described in a metaphor
taken from the cornfield. What they sow is merely wind, grain
light as air ; but the reaping is worse, even the destruction of the
whirlwind. Even if there is a result from the sowing of their
schemes, it does not come to maturity, to corn on the stalk. And
supposing it does so, there is no meal from it for the farmer to
use ; and even if he gets some, strangers or foes will have the
enjoyment of it. Just so, the exile will give the foreign nations
any results that may come from Israel's activities.

8. as a vessel wherein is no pleasure: i.e. for which there is
no use. It is a significant phrase in the light of Israel's later history, right up to the present day.

9. Part of Israel's policy was to seek alliance with Assyria, a
stupid, obstinate, and shifty thing to do. These are the charac-
teristics of the wild ass.

a wild ass alone by himself. These animals usually went in
herds, so this marks the strange conduct of one which runs off
into the desert in stubborn solitude ; cf. Gen. xvi. 12, where
Ishmael is compared to a wild ass.

hath hired lovers: or 'hath given love-gifts,' i.e. acted like
Menahem in sending presents to Assyria.

hire among the nations, now will I gather them; and they
begin to be minished by reason of the burden of the king
of princes. Because Ephraim hath multiplied altars to sin, 11
altars have been unto him to sin. Though I write for him 12
my law in ten thousand *precepts*, they are counted as a
strange thing. As for the sacrifices of mine offerings, they 13
sacrifice flesh and eat it; but the LORD accepteth them
not: now will he remember their iniquity, and visit their
sins; they shall return to Egypt. For Israel hath forgotten 14
his Maker, and builded palaces; and Judah hath multiplied

---

10. Although they wander off with such love-gifts, they will be
'gathered' into a captivity, and the Assyrian king has already laid
a burden on them which is reducing their powers.

But, following the LXX, the text has been altered by editors
so as to mean 'And they must cease for a while from the anointing
of kings and princes.'

11. Here the prophet turns to his second theme, their corrupted
and semi-idolatrous worship. What should have been for their
greater holiness, has become for their greater sin.

12. Although the *Torah* contains countless moral precepts as
well as ceremonial regulations, the former are regarded as having
no more influence than the words of a heathen outsider. The
verse when thus interpreted has some bearing on the existence of
a written law in Hosea's time. But an entirely different sense has
been suggested, viz.: 'Were I to write my laws by myriads, as
those of a stranger would they be accounted' (Harper, *op. cit.*
pp. 320–323).

13. The meaning of the first clause is obscure. It may mean
(1) that their sacrifices, which they think are offered to God, after
all are only offered to themselves as a dinner; or (2) that though
they carry out the correct ceremonial, they cannot be accepted
because of the unrepented sin that accompanies the sacrifice
(cf. Is. i. 13, 15, 'Bring no more vain oblations...your hands are
full of blood').

they shall return to Egypt: i.e. go into a captivity like the
ancient bondage before the exodus. It must be remembered that
it was still uncertain which of the two rival empires would absorb
them, Assyria or Egypt.

14. Besides their appeal to Assyria, and their trust in the outward appeal of offering sacrifices, the prophet condemns the trust
put in their fortifications, a trust soon to be falsified when Assyrian
invasion began.

builded palaces: the sense of the word is uncertain, but it is

fenced cities: but I will send a fire upon his cities, and it shall devour the castles thereof.

ix. 1-7 a. *The resulting exile will mean the ceasing of such things as harvest festivals.*

9 Rejoice not, O Israel, for joy, like the peoples ; for thou hast gone a whoring from thy God, thou hast loved hire
2 upon every cornfloor. The threshing-floor and the winepress
3 shall not feed them, and the new wine shall fail her. They shall not dwell in the LORD'S land; but Ephraim shall return to Egypt, and they shall eat unclean food in Assyria.

---

best explained in parallelism with the 'fenced cities' of the next clause.

The verse has been suspected for several reasons. (1) It is an imitation of Amos, who repeats the words 'I will send a fire' as the refrain of ch. i. (2) Also the idea of Jehovah as Israel's 'Maker' scarcely belongs to Hosea's time. (3) The section has a more fitting climax in *v.* 13.

ix. 1. The occasion of this prophecy seems to have been a harvest festival, in which Hosea checks the exuberance of the people's joy telling them that their feast is **like the peoples**, i.e. full of heathen elements, for it is an offering of thanks to the Baalim, and therefore an act of unfaithfulness to Israel's husband Jehovah. The result will be the ceasing of feasts through exile from their own land (*v.* 2 ff.).

thou hast loved hire. Israel in her harlotry accepts the corn as given by the Baalim, and her festival is an act of thanks to them instead of to Jehovah.

2. The resulting punishment will be the absence of corn harvest and vintage, for they will no longer enjoy their own land.

3. the Lord's land. This meant more to them than the words suggest to ourselves. For the prevailing idea, which Hosea himself reflects, was that each land had its own god, so that Jehovah would no longer be their God when they found themselves in a foreign land.

to Egypt...in Assyria. It was still uncertain which of the two empires which threatened Israel would actually absorb it. (See note on vii. 11-12.)

eat unclean food. It is not merely that they may have to eat food which was forbidden to the Israelites as unclean. For *v.* 4 implies that all their food would be unhallowed because they had not first offered some of it in thanksgiving at Jehovah's altars.

They shall not pour out wine *offerings* to the LORD, neither 4
shall they be pleasing unto him: their sacrifices shall be unto
them as the bread of mourners; all that eat thereof shall be
polluted: for their bread shall be for their appetite; it shall
not come into the house of the LORD. What will ye do in 5
the day of solemn assembly, and in the day of the feast of
the LORD? For, lo, they are gone away from destruction, 6
yet Egypt shall gather them up, Memphis shall bury them:
their pleasant things of silver, nettles shall possess them:
thorns shall be in their tents. The days of visitation are 7

---

4. It was no good making libations and sacrifices in a strange
land, for if they did, it could not please the God of Palestine.
This idea lingered (cf. Ezek. iv. 13), but Judah in exile learnt
that Jehovah was the only God, the Lord of the whole earth, and
so they finally passed from being henotheists, worshipping one
God, to a monotheism which proclaimed Him as the one God of
the world (see e.g. Is. xlii. 5, 6).

as the bread of mourners. The better rendering is that of the
R.V. mg. 'neither shall their sacrifices be pleasing unto him:
their bread shall be unto them as the bread of mourners.' Their
food shall be like the food eaten during the seven days of
mourning for a dead man, which made those who shared it
polluted, and therefore unable to make offerings to God. Their
food in exile could only satisfy themselves, without satisfying
Jehovah, as it *might* be doing now, if there were no heathenish
element in their feasts of harvest.

5. There would then be no possibility of keeping holy their
sabbaths, new moons, and harvest festivals. It will be remembered
that their three great festivals were all connected with the harvest.

6. from destruction: i.e. from their own destroyed and de-
vastated land. But the words are awkward, and if Wellhausen's
conjecture of 'to Assyria' be accepted, the thought agrees with
that of *v.* 3, which combines Assyria with Egypt as a possible land
of exile. In that case *yet* must be omitted.

Memphis shall bury them. Memphis, the capital of lower
(i.e. Northern) Egypt, was always a noted burying-place, and
is appropriately connected here with Israel's death and decay.

their pleasant things, etc. The picture is of the land left
behind. Their treasure-houses (or perhaps their idols of silver)
will be overgrown with nettles, and their 'dwellings' will give
place to thorns, cf. Isaiah's similar description (xxxiv. 13-15):
'Thorns shall come up in her palaces, nettles and thistles in the
fortresses thereof.'

come, the days of recompence are come; Israel shall know it:

7 b-9. *A parenthesis explaining and justifying his own position.*

the prophet is a fool, the man that hath the spirit is mad, for the multitude of thine iniquity, and because the enmity
8 is great. Ephraim *was* a watchman with my God: as for the prophet, a fowler's snare is in all his ways, *and* enmity
9 in the house of his God. They have deeply corrupted themselves, as in the days of Gibeah: he will remember their iniquity, he will visit their sins.

---

7. Israel shall know it: or 'Israel shall know,' i.e. there will be no doubt about recognising the calamity when it comes. The words are best taken with what precedes.

7 b–9. These verses are difficult and obscure, and editors, giving up the text as hopeless, have tried to re-write them. It seems best to take them as a parenthesis, suggested by his last assertion that some day they shall all 'know it,' and not himself only. If the preceding section was a prophecy uttered at a harvest festival, the indignation may well be imagined with which his words were greeted. He now explains that if prophecy seems to have gone 'mad,' it is the result of the national corruption which he has to rebuke. The corruption is there, and will certainly be punished, however they treat Jehovah's prophet.

7 b. the prophet is a fool: these words, coming from the mouths of those who keep festival, he allows to be in some sense true, but caused by the people's own sins, and by their attitude of hostility. A less likely explanation is that he is here referring to the false prophets.

8. Ephraim *was* a watchman with my God. If there is any sense in this translation, it must mean that the whole nation was meant to be God's watchman. Harper ingeniously links the words with what precedes, and reads 'Enmity exists towards Ephraim's watchman,' i.e. the prophet (*op. cit.* p. 333). Melville Scott reads, 'Ephraim setteth an ambush against the people of my God' (*op. cit.* p. 160).

If the reading of the R.V. mg. be taken, the words may then mean that the nation, in thus treating Hosea, is actually 'watching against' his God, as well as laying snares for the prophet himself, and shewing their hostility to him even in the house of his God.

9. as in the days of Gibeah: a favourite allusion of Hosea's to express the immoral side of their national corruption. The

10-17. Their punishment will fit their immoral sins.

I found Israel like grapes in the wilderness; I saw your 10
fathers as the firstripe in the fig tree at her first season :
but they came to Baal-peor, and consecrated themselves
unto the shameful thing, and became abominable like that
which they loved. As for Ephraim, their glory shall fly 11
away like a bird : there shall be no birth, and none with
child, and no conception. Though they bring up their 12
children, yet will I bereave them, that there be not a man
left : yea, woe also to them when I depart from them !
Ephraim, like as I have seen Tyre, is planted in a pleasant 13

---

story of Judges xix. is altogether disgusting, and the painful part
of it is that the rest of the tribe of Benjamin actually went to war
in defence of the depraved citizens of Gibeah. See also x. 9.

10. Editors are not agreed as to where a new section should
begin. Although this verse with its 'abominations' carries
on the thought of the corruption 'as in the days of Gibeah' of
v. 9, it states the sin for which the punishment of a declining
birth-rate is unfolded in *vv.* 11-17.

Israel was once as full of promise to Jehovah as a vine espied
by a traveller in the desert, or the first crop of figs in early summer,
but the promise had been utterly falsified.

they came to Baal-peor: an historical allusion to a corruption
even earlier than Gibeah, viz. their attraction to a Moabite Baal,
which took place when they had scarcely entered the promised
land (Numb. xxv. 3).

the shameful thing. Heb. 'shame,' such worship being utterly
immoral.

and became abominable, etc.: i.e. the objects of their immoral
worship infected their own lives.

11. The first result of the decay of morality in a nation is in
the shrinkage of its population through a decline in the birth-rate.
This may be a truism now, but G. A. Smith writes 'I am unaware
of any earlier moralist in any literature who traced the effects of
national licentiousness in a diminishing population' (*op. cit.* p.
283).

12. Their punishment goes further : even the children which
are born shall not grow up, when God finally leaves His people.

13. A third step in their punishment ; even if the children grow
up, they will fall before their foes.

like as I have seen Tyre, etc.: i.e. in a state of proud prosperity,

place: but Ephraim shall bring out his children to the
14 slayer. Give them, O LORD: what wilt thou give? give
15 them a miscarrying womb and dry breasts. All their
wickedness is in Gilgal; for there I hated them: because
of the wickedness of their doings I will drive them out of
mine house: I will love them no more; all their princes
16 are revolters. Ephraim is smitten, their root is dried up,
they shall bear no fruit: yea, though they bring forth, yet
17 will I slay the beloved fruit of their womb. My God will
cast them away, because they did not hearken unto him:
and they shall be wanderers among the nations.

---

and perhaps of boasting at their large population (cf. x. 1, 'Israel is
a luxuriant vine'). But the text is quite uncertain. The LXX reads
'Ephraim's children as I have seen are appointed for capture.'

14. This is not to be regarded as 'a charitable prayer' that there
may be none to suffer such things. Rather does the prophet actually
pray for the coming of Jehovah's punishment of childlessness.
The extent of the calamity can scarcely be appreciated except by
Jews. The Bible is full of stories which illustrate the necessity of
having sons to perpetuate a man's own life as well as his family,
and of the 'reproach among men' which befell the childless wife.

15. The ancient sanctuary of Gilgal had become the head-
quarters of their immoralities, which would lead to their exile
from the land (if this be the meaning of 'mine house,' as is suggested
in the note on viii. 1).

But some see in the whole passage a reference to child-sacrifice,
as the sin directly responsible for the punishment. Melville Scott
suggests that this verse affords evidence of its existence in Gilgal,
and that it is mentioned as present a few years later in Judah (*op. cit.*
p. 61). But all this is scarcely proven.

all their princes are revolters. There is a play on the two
words. Horton suggests 'their princes are prancers,' like refrac-
tory animals. This new thought comes strangely here, unless, as
so often happens, the example of immorality was set by the
nation's ruling class.

16. Harper places this after *v.* 11, because it returns to the punishment of childlessness. But it is Hosea's manner to revert to
what has already been treated of. In any case, there is a series
of clauses like those of *vv.* 11 and 12. Their fruit is dead, but
even if not, no fruit will come; and if it does, destruction will
befall; and if not that, then exile.

3. A SUMMARY OF THEIR SINS, WHICH ARE LEADING
   THEM TO DESPAIR, AND TO PUNISHMENT AS SURE
   AS THAT OF BENJAMIN FOR THE SIN AT GIBEAH.
   X. 1–10.

x. 1–4. *Altars, kings, and treaties all bring punishment.*

Israel is a luxuriant vine, which putteth forth his fruit: **10**
according to the multitude of his fruit he hath multiplied
his altars; according to the goodness of his land they have
made goodly pillars. Their heart is divided; now shall **2**
they be found guilty: he shall smite their altars, he shall
spoil their pillars. Surely now shall they say, We have no **3**
king: for we fear not the LORD; and the king, what can
he do for us? They speak *vain* words, swearing falsely in **4**
making covenants: therefore judgement springeth up as
hemlock in the furrows of the field.

5–10. *Calf worship will cause despair at last.*

The inhabitants of Samaria shall be in terror for the calves **5**

---

x. 1. Another division of the book seems to begin here,
although the earlier verses repeat the sins already condemned.

The facilities of worship have kept pace with the population
and the prosperity of the land (for the **luxuriant vine**, see note
on x. 13), but all in vain, because of the taint of heathenism.

pillars. See note on v. 4.

2. Their heart is divided: i.e. between Jehovah and Baal. But
it may be 'smooth' (as R.V. mg.), i.e. slippery, deceitful.

3. Their feeble kings are unworthy of the name, and unable
to help them when the crisis comes. From their heavenly King
they have already turned. But they would not have acknowledged
that they did not fear Him. Hence the unnecessary surmise that
the words are later, after the time of the exile.

4. A third item in the indictment is that they have broken their
covenants with Jehovah. Punishment will spring up as inevitably
as weeds in a cornfield. Or are they covenants with the nations,
as in *v.* 6? Melville Scott thinks that the reference is to Hoshea's
refusal to pay his tribute to Shalmaneser, and that there was 'no
king' because the latter had imprisoned him (*op. cit.* p. 63).

5. At length they will realise the futility of the calf-worship

of Beth-aven: for the people thereof shall mourn over it,
and the priests thereof that rejoiced over it, for the glory
6 thereof, because it is departed from it. It also shall be
carried unto Assyria for a present to king Jareb: Ephraim
shall receive shame, and Israel shall be ashamed of his
7 own counsel. *As for* Samaria, her king is cut off, as foam
8 upon the water. The high places also of Aven, the sin of
Israel, shall be destroyed: the thorn and the thistle shall
come up on their altars; and they shall say to the mountains,
9 Cover us; and to the hills, Fall on us. O Israel, thou hast

---

begun by Jeroboam long ago. The plural **calves** is unexpected,
unless the number of them at Beth-el (for Beth-aven see note on
iv. 15) had been increased. If we follow the LXX and read 'calf,'
it explains the singular 'it,' which occurs three times in the rest
of the verse.

the priests. The word is used in scorn, for it is elsewhere only
applied to the idolatrous priests (as in 2 Kings xxiii. 5).

that rejoiced has been emended to 'shall howl' or 'shall
writhe.'

because it is departed from it: i.e. the glory of the calf is
done away.

6. The golden calf itself will have to be paid as tribute to
Assyria, a policy which will cause national shame.

king Jareb. See note on v. 13.

7. as foam. This is the Rabbinic explanation of a rare word,
but a better meaning is a chip or twig (as R.V. mg.), which is
tossed along helpless in the waters.

8. Aven: i.e. Beth-aven, the perversion of Beth-el. See note
on iv. 15. It is 'Aven,' and not the 'high places,' which Hosea
regards as the **sin of Israel,** but these latter words may be a
gloss.

the thistle. The Hebrew word is only used in Gen. iii. 18, of
the original curse upon the land.

they shall say to the mountains, etc.: i.e. the hill-tops will
now be bare of altars, and instead of their use for seeking divine
help, the only appeal to them now is to cover their shame and to
hide them from punishment. The words are familiar from their
N.T. use, once in our Lord's prediction of the destruction of
Jerusalem (Lk. xxiii. 30) and again in a vision of the judgement
day (Rev. vi. 16). Here they reveal the despair to which Israel
will be reduced.

sinned from the days of Gibeah: there they stood; that
the battle against the children of iniquity should not overtake them in Gibeah. When it is my desire, I will chastise 10
them; and the peoples shall be gathered against them,
when they are bound to their two transgressions.

4. THEY HAD THOUGHT TO COMBINE WITH THEIR
INIQUITIES THEIR LIGHTER DUTIES TOWARDS JE-
HOVAH, AND MUST THEREFORE NOW BEAR HIS
CHASTISEMENT. x. 11–15.

11–12. *There was a harder discipline than they
had undergone.*

And Ephraim is an heifer that is taught, that loveth to 11

---

9. from the days of Gibeah. Already (ix. 9) Hosea has referred
to the sin of Benjamin in Judges xix. This must therefore be the
meaning here. Some have objected that it was only one tribe
that sinned, and not all 'Israel,' but the taint of corruption entered them, and so the general sin of later days could be traced
back to it. Wellhausen thinks that the sin lay in founding a
monarchy under Saul, since Gibeah was Saul's city.

there they stood, etc. The meaning is hard to discover. As
the words stand they picture the Benjamites stubbornly facing
the attack of the other tribes, in order that they may not suffer
at their hands for their iniquity. Such was Israel's present stub-
bornness against God. For various emendations, see Harper, *op.
cit.* p. 351.

10. when they are bound to their two transgressions. Their
fall will be the result of two sins, from which they have been
unable to free themselves. But what are the two sins? Many
answers have been given, e.g. (1) the two calves, in Beth-el and
Dan. (But the transgression was the same for both.) (2) Apostasy from God and acceptance of idols. (3) Their revolt from
Jehovah their God and David their king (Cheyne, *op. cit.* p. 104).
This seems best, and accords with iii. 5, which predicts two returns, to 'the LORD their God, and David their king,' a healing
of the schism caused by the revolt of the northern tribes under
Jeroboam.

11. The heifer has been broken in, but prefers the easy work
of treading the corn, with the chance of feeding upon it during
the process (Deut. xxv. 4). There is harder work in store, drawing,
ploughing, and harrowing. Even so, God's people preferred an

tread out *the corn*; but I have passed over upon her fair
neck: I will set a rider on Ephraim; Judah shall plow,
12 Jacob shall break his clods. Sow to yourselves in righteousness, reap according to mercy; break up your fallow
ground: for it is time to seek the LORD, till he come and
rain righteousness upon you.

13-15. *They will now reap as they have sown.*

13 Ye have plowed wickedness, ye have reaped iniquity; ye
have eaten the fruit of lies: for thou didst trust in thy way,
14 in the multitude of thy mighty men. Therefore shall a
tumult arise among thy people, and all thy fortresses shall
be spoiled, as Shalman spoiled Beth-arbel in the day of

---

easy service, 'spiritual results, without a spiritual discipline'
(G. A. Smith), but the yoke was in store for them, and the hard
discipline of the exile.

but I have passed over. Either, I have been sparing, with a
kindness which has been abused, or I have put a yoke upon.

I will set a rider. This is the usual meaning of the Heb. word,
but it can also mean 'make to draw,' which is a much better sense
here.

12. The metaphor is carried on in this tender appeal. The
temptation comes to the indolent husbandman, as well as to his
heifer, to scamp the processes of husbandry. Unless the clods
are broken up, the rain will be of no use. Even so, if God's grace
is to be upon Israel, they must make a change in their evil habits,
and allow their religion to reform their lives.

13-15. These verses conclude the section, summing up both
their offence and its punishment. The reaping is in striking contrast with that of the preceding verse.

13. thou didst trust in thy way: i.e. in their own ways,
instead of God's. Some editors follow the LXX, and read 'in
thy chariots,' which makes a better parallel with 'thy mighty men.'
But the latter may refer to help from *foreign* powers. If this is
so, it explains the plural of 'thy peoples' (Heb. and R.V. mg.)
in *v.* 14.

14. as Shalman spoiled Beth-arbel. The reference is obscure,
and many surmises have been made. Beth-arbel is almost certainly the Arbela near the lake of Galilee, mentioned in 1 Macc.
ix. 2. But who was Shalman? (1) The Moabite king Salamaner,
who paid tribute to Tiglath-Pileser, and may well have invaded
Galilee. (2) Shalmaneser III of Assyria, whose expedition against

battle: the mother was dashed in pieces with her children.
So shall Beth-el do unto you because of your great wicked- 15
ness: at daybreak shall the king of Israel be utterly cut off.

C. THE PENALTY OF IGNORING THE FATHERLY
    LOVE OF GOD. xi. 1–xii. 1.

xi. 1–4. *Israel has rejected the fatherliness and
tenderness of Jehovah.*

When Israel was a child, then I loved him, and called 11

Damascus, a generation previous to Hosea, may have extended
farther south. (3) Shalmaneser IV, who became king in 727 B.C.,
and began the final siege of Samaria. But there is no other
proof that Hosea's words were so late. (4) Zalmunna, the Midianite
invader in the days of Gideon (Jerubbaal). This may be suggested
by the LXX reading 'Jerubbaal' instead of Shalman, but the fact
that Zalmunna was defeated and slain makes this explanation
unlikely (see Judges vi. and vii.). The first explanation seems the
best.

15. So shall Beth-el do: i.e. the sin which centred in Beth-el
will cause their fall. Some read 'So shall it be done unto you at
Beth-el' (as R.V. mg.), others emend to 'So shall I do unto you,
O house of Israel' (Beth-Israel), following the LXX.

at daybreak: in a figurative sense, 'as suddenly as the dawn,
the night of their sinful sleep being now far spent.

xi. 1 ff. We have seen (Introd. pp. 11–13) that one great contribution which Hosea made to the world's spiritual and theological ideas, was his new conception of Israel's God as full, not
only of righteousness, as Amos had already proclaimed, but of a
father's tender love for His people. This appears most plainly in
the climax of ch. xiv., but ch. xi. is very like it, and is the most
pathetic of all Hosea's prophecies, for it is mingled with the
thought, not of restoration, but of rejection on man's part.

1. called my son out of Egypt. This of course refers to the
Exodus, but the beautiful thought is that it was a poor little
nation, not only in its infancy, but in slavery in Egypt, that
God chose to be His own child, and tenderly guided to the land
that was to be theirs. Another and still more beautiful rendering
is 'called him to be my son.' The phrase is familiar from its use
by S. Matthew (ii. 15), who sees in the return of the infant Saviour
from Egypt a fresh fulfilment of the words. And indeed the
prophet's words have an abiding significance, and reveal God's
Fatherhood in every age.

2 my son out of Egypt. As they called them, so they went
from them: they sacrificed unto the Baalim, and burned
3 incense to graven images. Yet I taught Ephraim to go;
I took them on my arms; but they knew not that I healed
4 them. I drew them with cords of a man, with bands of
love; and I was to them as they that take off the yoke on
their jaws, and I laid meat before them.

5-11. *The punishment of exile must result, but Jehovah
can scarcely bear to execute the punishment.*

5 He shall not return into the land of Egypt; but the

---

2. In spite of Jehovah's fatherhood from the beginning, they
turned from Him to Baals and idols.

3. Israel was like a little child whose father teaches it to walk,
but who does not realise his tender care. When the little one is
tired, he takes it up in his arms.

4. The picture changes from the father's care for his child to
the merciful man's care for his beast. It is not the young heifer
which hates the yoke, but the team of patient oxen toiling uphill.
It is not just a beast's harness that is used, but an affectionate and
almost human drawing by the **cords of a man.** The man in charge
goes to their heads and moves the chafing yoke farther forward
on their necks, and delights to give them their feed afterwards
with loving hands. This homely but beautiful simile brings home
another side of God's tenderness, when man is no longer in leading
strings, but harnessed to the hard work of life, and 'we look up,
not so much for the fatherliness as for the gentleness and humanity
of our God' (G. A. Smith, *op. cit.* p. 296). This explanation of
the verse suits well with the language Hosea uses elsewhere in
which he compares Israel to an heifer (iv. 16 and x. 11). It is
strange therefore that some commentators give it up as hopelessly
corrupt, and proceed to emend it. Melville Scott takes it as a con-
tinuation of the previous verse, and renders 'I was to them as they
that lift up a babe to their bosom, and I bent down unto him and
carried him' (*op. cit.* p. 144). It is true that the word which the
R.V. translates by 'take off' means 'lift up,' but that meaning
has been given it in the above explanation.

5-7. The change from tenderness to wrath is a sudden one,
the necessity for the Father to punish His erring children comes
naturally between the tender promise of *vv.* 1-4 and the piteous
appeal from the Father's heart in *vv.* 8-9.

5. He shall not return into the land of Egypt. This a place
where a trifling emendation is really necessary. The point is that

Assyrian shall be his king, because they refused to return. And the sword shall fall upon his cities, and shall consume 6 his bars, and devour *them*, because of their own counsels. And my people are bent to backsliding from me : though 7 they call them to *him that is* on high, none at all will exalt *him*. How shall I give thee up, Ephraim? *how* shall I 8 deliver thee, Israel? how shall I make thee as Admah? *how* shall I set thee as Zeboim? mine heart is turned

because Israel would not return to Jehovah, exile must befall them, though (as in ix. 3) Hosea is uncertain whether it is Egypt or Assyria that will absorb them. So the **not** must be omitted, or the sentence made interrogative, as 'Shall he not return, etc.?' For **but** read 'and' in the second part of the verse.

6. shall consume his bars. The word translated 'bars' is of uncertain meaning. It may mean (1) 'fortresses,' as in Jer. li. 30, or (2) 'branches' as the A.V. renders, or (3) 'mighty men,' or 'boasters,' as in Jer. l. 36. This last meaning accords best with what follows, for **their own counsels** may refer to those who led the parties which favoured either Egypt or Assyria.

7. No one has been able to make much sense of this verse, except by drastic emendation. The R.V. transl. means that they are twisted aside by their sinfulness, so that although they call each other to honour God with their lips, they fail to exalt Him in their hearts.

But the Heb. only has 'though they call them upwards,' which may refer to the prophets, or to the leaders (perhaps the 'mighty men' suggested in the note on *v.* 6) who encourage a debased Jehovah worship, but do not exalt the people thereby.

8–11. G. A. Smith's words (*op. cit.* p. 297) are the best comment on these verses. 'There follows the greatest passage in Hosea—deepest if not highest in his book—the bieaking forth of that exhau-tless mercy of the Most High, which no sin of man can bar back nor wear out.' In what has been called 'The remorse of God,' His divine Heart bursting with tenderness for the disobedient child, He cries out that He cannot hand them over to irrevocable destruction.

8. as Admah...as Zeboim : two of the cities of the plain, mentioned along with Sodom and Gomorrah in Gen. xiv. 2. Although Gen. xix. does not mention their overthrow with that of the two last named, we may take it that such was the beliel of later times, as is shewn by Deut. xxix. 23. Hosea evidently had sources of information about the early history which are not in Genesis. See Introd. p. 16. Sodom and Gomorrah are similarly used as examples and warnings by Amos (iv. 11).

9 within me, my compassions are kindled together. I will
not execute the fierceness of mine anger, I will not return
to destroy Ephraim: for I am God, and not man; the
Holy One in the midst of thee: and I will not enter into
10 the city. They shall walk after the LORD, who shall roar
like a lion: for he shall roar, and the children shall come
11 trembling from the west. They shall come trembling as a
bird out of Egypt, and as a dove out of the land of Assyria:
and I will make them to dwell in their houses, saith the
LORD.

12–xii. 1. *Israel is false and deceitful in every way.*

12 Ephraim compasseth me about with falsehood, and the
house of Israel with deceit: but Judah yet ruleth with God,
12 and is faithful with the Holy One. Ephraim feedeth on

---

9. I am God, and not man: i.e. though He has human attri-
butes, His anger with their sin does not divert His perpetual love
and mercy, as it would in the case of a man.

I will not enter into the city: i.e. for punishment, as in the
case of the cities of the plain. But the words are obscure, and
emendations give (1) 'I am not willing to consume,' or (2) 'I will
not enter in anger.'

10–11. The voice of God, awe-inspiring and heard from afar,
like that of a lion (cf. Amos iii. 8) will call them out of all the
places whither they have been driven in exile. Their speed will
be as that of birds, when they return like homing doves. But are
the words Hosea's, or a plainer promise inserted after the exile?

10. from the west: i.e. the sea, and the coast lands and 'islands
of the sea' (cf. Is. xi. 11) of which Hosea's knowledge would be
vague. Some would emend to 'from their captivity,' or 'from the
nations.'

12. This verse certainly belongs, and in the Heb. is assigned, to
the next chapter. The change of thought is complete, and Israel's
unfaithfulness again becomes the dominant note, but Jehovah
still speaks, not with future promise, but with present reproach.

but Judah yet ruleth with God. The commendation of the
southern kingdom is entirely out of place here, even apart from
the language of xii. 2. Either a later Judaean writer has added
the words, or they really bear an adverse sense, such as that of
the R.V. mg. 'and Judah is yet unstedfast with God, and with
the Holy One who is faithful.'

xii. 1. Part of their falseness to God lay in seeking foreign

wind, and followeth after the east wind: he continually multiplieth lies and desolation; and they make a covenant with Assyria, and oil is carried into Egypt.

D. IN THEIR DECEIT THEY ARE LIKE THEIR FATHER JACOB, WHOSE HISTORY IS A LESSON FOR THE PRESENT. xii. 2–14.

2–6. *Episodes in Jacob's history.*

The LORD hath also a controversy with Judah, and will 2

---

alliances; these were as vain as the **wind**, and indeed utterly withering, like the sirocco that came from the south-east.

lies and desolation: or, better, 'lies and fraud,' as the LXX gives.

oil is carried into Egypt. There is the usual combination of the two alternative conquerors. Oil was an important product of Palestine, and would naturally be exported to Egypt, which was without it.

2–14. The division of the chapters has already proved untrustworthy, since xi. 12 is so closely linked with xii. 1, and a fresh theme seems to begin at xii. 2. For the lesson of Jacob's history stands unique in the book, and it is the mention of his name in *v.* 2 that introduces the subject. The analysis of this section is made more difficult because in all probability the verses are not in their original order. After giving two episodes of Jacob's history in *v.* 4, it is strange that he does not give the third until *v.* 12. As this last does not fit well with what precedes it, it does not seem unreasonable to rearrange the chapter, a course which has already been resorted to in the case of chs. ii. and iii. This is very different from the wholesale emendation and excision which has played such havoc with the text of the book. The lesson of Jacob seems to be that he was a supplanter, and full of deceit; an unfavourable estimate of a great patriarch, which may well have shocked those who read the book, and caused someone to insert a defence of him in the text. Supposing that *v.* 3a ('In the womb he took his brother by the heel') was followed by *v.* 12 ('And Jacob fled into the field of Aram, and Israel served for a wife, and for a wife he kept sheep'), someone might have inserted between them the contents of *vv.* 3b–6, recording his wrestling with the angel and his finding God at Beth-el, and proceeding to give a pious recommendation to follow his example and turn to God, and wait on Him continually. Melville Scott puts it thus: 'Quite obviously there was now no room for them where they originally stood, and room had to be found for them some-

punish Jacob according to his ways; according to his
3 doings will he recompense him. In the womb he took his
brother by the heel: and in his manhood he had power
4 with God: yea, he had power over the angel, and prevailed:
he wept, and made supplication unto him: he found him
5 at Beth-el, and there he spake with us; even the LORD,
6 the God of hosts; the LORD is his memorial. Therefore
turn thou to thy God: keep mercy and judgement, and
wait on thy God continually.

---

where else. The only place to put them was further down, and
apparently the words (*v.* 13) 'by a prophet the LORD brought
Israel up out of Egypt, and by a prophet was he preserved' were
placed with them from the superficial resemblance which they
afford to 'Israel served for a wife, and for a wife he shepherded'
(*op. cit.* p. 71).

In this commentary the traditional order is followed for the sake
of convenience.

2. a controversy with Judah. The word needed is 'Israel,' and
it is better to substitute it for 'Judah,' which has just occurred
in xi. 12, and might easily be repeated by mistake.

will punish Jacob. Hosea shews the same bold and critical
attitude towards a great patriarch as towards the schism of the
northern kingdom (see i. 4 and viii. 4).

3-6. See previous note on 2-14 for the probability that these
words are a later gloss. Jacob began to be a supplanter from the
moment of his birth, when he tried to supplant the elder twin
Esau (Gen. xxv. 26).

3. he had power with God: this anticipates the mention of his
wrestling in *v.* 4.

4. It is curious that the scene at Peniel should be placed before
that at Beth-el. For the former, see Gen. xxxii. 29. It is used to
shew the ambitious character of Jacob, already manifested at his
birth. We are not told elsewhere that **he wept**, so that Hosea
shews here, as elsewhere, independent historical knowledge.

and there he spake with us: i.e. to Jacob, who was identified
with his descendants. But such an explanation is forced, and it
is better to read 'with him.' In the case of the vision at Beth-el
and its sequel, it does not seem to be adduced as a matter of
blame, although, to our modern ideas, it is not for man to make
bargains with God (Gen. xxviii. 20, 21).

5. his memorial: i.e. his name.

6. This sudden exhortation can only be suggested by the
behaviour of Jacob. But to imitate his kindness and justice

7–14. Failure of Israel in later times to learn the lesson.

He is a trafficker, the balances of deceit are in his hand: 7
he loveth to oppress. And Ephraim said, Surely I am 8
become rich, I have found me wealth: in all my labours
they shall find in me none iniquity that were sin. But I 9
am the LORD thy God from the land of Egypt; I will yet
again make thee to dwell in tents, as in the days of the
solemn feast. I have also spoken unto the prophets, and 10

---

towards men, and his faithfulness to God, does not agree
with the estimate of Jacob in the previous verses. Hence the
likelihood that these words are a pious gloss.

7. Who is here referred to? There are two lines of interpretation. (1) The reference is in the first place to Jacob, who shewed
deceit throughout, even by his cheating of Laban when serving
for a wife. (2) It is Israel of later days that proved deceitful. In
either case, the point of the verse is that in spite of spiritual
privileges, unscrupulous money-making was the ruling passion.

He is **a trafficker**: rather, as in R.V. mg., he is denounced as a
mere 'Canaanite' in spirit. To call Israel 'Canaan' was the
most crushing of indictments, for the name of the original inhabitants of the land stood for heathen baseness, and point is added
if the word is in the vocative case. 'Thou Canaan!' But as the
Canaanites provided the cities with their merchandise, the name
had become equivalent to **trafficker** or 'merchant,' and is so used
e.g. in Ezek. xvii. 4. This justifies the translation of the R.V.

to oppress: or rather 'to defraud' (as R.V. mg.) which suits
better with the character described.

8. Israel is represented as defending the money-getting; it
is not denied, but the sin of it cannot be brought home to him.
He is like the unscrupulous trader who argues that he has kept
within the law, and fails to realise that there are higher ideals of
living.

9. Ever since the Exodus they had been God's children (xi. 1),
and as the wanderings of the wilderness had been a blessing as
well as a discipline (as the feast of Tabernacles reminded them
year by year), so would it be with the fresh wanderings of the
exile.

as in the days of the solemn feast. Some would emend this
clause, on the ground that the connecting of the feast with the
tents of the wilderness was a later idea.

10. The connexion of this verse with its context is difficult to
find. The word **also** suggests that, besides speaking to them

I have multiplied visions; and by the ministry of the
11 prophets have I used similitudes. Is Gilead iniquity? they
are altogether vanity; in Gilgal they sacrifice bullocks:
yea, their altars are as heaps in the furrows of the field.
12 And Jacob fled into the field of Aram, and Israel served
13 for a wife, and for a wife he kept *sheep*. And by a prophet
the LORD brought Israel up out of Egypt, and by a prophet
14 was he preserved. Ephraim hath provoked to anger most

---

through the experience of the wilderness, God also spake by the
prophets. Their **similitudes** would include both Hosea's own
message as illustrated by his relations with Gomer in chs. i–iii.,
and such parables as those of Nathan (2 Sam. xii. 1 ff.) and
Isaiah (v. 1 ff.)

11. In spite of the prophets, the whole land is sunk in sin and
the perversion of religious worship, whether Gilead on the east
of Jordan or Gilgal on the west. So their very altars will be
laid low. This is the sense of the words as they stand, but most
editors give up the passage as hopeless.

as heaps in the furrows: i.e. like the stones which the farmer
puts in piles as he clears the land of them.

12. For the probability that this verse is misplaced, and
belongs to *v*. 3, see note at the beginning of ch. xii. In that connexion it further illustrates Jacob's deceit and its results.

If it is retained in this place, there has been suggested, in his
journey eastward and return with a beloved wife as the result of
his discipline, 'a gleam of encouragement to the guilty nation
which is to go into the desert and dwell in tents again' (Horton,
op. cit. p. 66). But is it meant for encouragement? May we not
rather say that the mention of the wilderness, both in connexion
with the exodus and the exile, reminds Hosea that Jacob himself
had an experience of the wilderness, and although he did bring
back a wife, he had to spend years of hard work to do it, and
was paid back by Laban for his own deceit?

the field of Aram: a translation of Paddan-aram of Gen.
xxviii. 2.

13. If *v*. 12 is out of place, and *v*. 11 is hopeless, then *v*. 13 is
brought closer to *v*. 10, which it echoes by its double mention of
the word 'prophet.' The words of course refer to Moses, who
saved Israel once in the wilderness. Horton calls this 'another
gleam of hope in coming punishment,' i.e. another Moses may
arise to save them in the wilderness of exile.

and by a prophet was he preserved: or 'shepherded.' For
Moses as a 'prophet,' see Deut. xviii. 15.

bitterly: therefore shall his blood be left upon him, and his reproach shall his Lord return unto him.

E. THE LAST JUDGEMENT OF ISRAEL. xiii. 1-16.

xiii. 1-3. *Baal is the cause of their overthrow.*

When Ephraim spake, there was trembling; he exalted 13 himself in Israel: but when he offended in Baal, he died. And now they sin more and more, and have made them 2 molten images of their silver, even idols according to their own understanding, all of them the work of the craftsmen: they say of them, Let the men that sacrifice kiss the calves.

---

14. This verse seems to carry on the thought of *v.* 11.

shall his blood be left upon him. The bloodshed which he has committed will be a proof of his guilt, and God will requite him for the insult which his idolatry has put upon Him.

ch. xiii. In the section which begins here this ray of hope is no longer seen. It is true that the words of *v.* 14 have been used by S. Paul as a glorious promise of victory over death, but it is more likely than not that this is the reverse of their original significance. But the possibilities of restoration hinted at in ch. xii. reappear as certainties, when the night of punishment is past, in ch. xiv. Meanwhile ch. xiii. sums up all Hosea's warnings, in one final but despairing call to repentance.

xiii. 1. When Ephraim spake, etc. The great central tribe of Ephraim, so often named as representing the whole northern kingdom, had commanded the respect of all the rest; but it meant spiritual death when he introduced Baal worship. If there was a special moment in his history when he offended, it was either through 'the sin of Jeroboam the son of Nebat, who made Israel to sin' and inaugurated the calf-worship, or the introduction of Baal worship by the house of Omri.

there was trembling. Cheyne and Scott prefer the A.V. translation 'When Ephraim spake trembling, he exalted himself in Israel,' which refers to the long past when he still humbled himself before Jehovah, and therefore was exalted.

2. more and more. Perverted Jehovah worship led by degrees to sheer idolatry.

Let the men that sacrifice kiss the calves. This appears to be an order, given in connexion with calf-worship, which is held up to ridicule. The phrase literally means 'sacrificers of men,' and

3 **Therefore** they shall be as the morning cloud, and **as the**
dew that passeth early away, as the chaff that is driven
with the whirlwind out of the threshing-floor, and as the
smoke out of the chimney.

4-9. They failed to recognise their true Saviour.

4 **Yet** I am the LORD thy God from the land of Egypt; and
thou shalt know no god but me, and beside me there is
5 **no** saviour. I did know thee in the wilderness, in the land
6 **of great** drought. According to their pasture, so were they
filled; they were filled, and their heart was exalted: there-
7 **fore** have they forgotten me. Therefore am I unto them
8 **as a lion**: as a leopard will I watch by the way: I will
meet them as a bear that is bereaved of her whelps, and
will rend the caul of their heart: and there will I devour
9 **them** like a lion; the wild beast shall tear them. It is thy

---

so some would take it as actually referring to human sacrifice.
Against this it may be urged (1) that there is no other indication
in Hosea of so horrible a custom in connexion with Israel's worship (though it was known shortly afterwards), (2) that the
prophet would hardly mention it so lightly without any direct
condemnation. The words more likely mean 'those among men
who sacrifice,' and the order is quoted to shew the absurdity of
living men paying homage to mere molten calves.

3. The language of vi. 4 is repeated. As their religion has
ended in nothingness, so will they themselves.

the smoke out of the chimney. This passage has been taken
as the only proof that the Hebrews had chimneys in the roof.
But Harper translates it 'windows' as in Gen. vii. 11, etc. (*op. cit.*
p. 397).

4. 'It is not enough to recognize God as Saviour; He must
be recognized as the only Saviour' (Horton, *op. cit.* p. 68).

Hosea has already described in viii. 14 the hardening and
debasing influence of prosperity upon God's people.

7. The God who was really their Saviour is turned to be their
destroyer.

as a leopard will I watch by the way: the Heb. will bear
this meaning but it also can mean 'as a leopard on the way to
Assyria.' This rendering is that of the LXX, and it enables us
to explain **there** in *v.* 8.

9. They brought their own destruction by turning their backs

destruction, O Israel, that *thou art* against me, against
thy help.

10–16. *Nothing can help nor save them now.*

Where now is thy king, that he may save thee in all thy 10
cities? and thy judges, of whom thou saidst, Give me a
king and princes? I have given thee a king in mine anger, 11
and have taken him away in my wrath. The iniquity of 12
Ephraim is bound up: his sin is laid up in store. The sorrows 13
of a travailing woman shall come upon him: he is an unwise
son; for it is time he should not tarry in the place of the

---

on Him who would be their Saviour. But the text is very uncertain.

10–11. Among the other saviours now powerless to help them
is the monarchy. The nation had demanded a king long ago,
and had reason to be sorry that their prayer was granted, whereby
they had shewn their lack of trust in Jehovah as their king.
Since then kings had come and gone, and for the last few years
one had succeeded another in a series of usurpations, but such
changes were only marks of the wrath of their true Saviour.

10. Give me a king: this may refer (1) to the original demand
made of Samuel, which one of the narratives taught men to regard
as sinful; or (2) to the divided monarchy, and the support given
to Jeroboam.

11. Horton (*op. cit.* p. 11) sees a reference to the giving of a
first king in Jeroboam, and the taking away of the last one in
Hoshea (in 722 B.C.). But it is better still to refer Hosea's language to the anarchy of 743–734 B.C.

12. Their sin cannot now be undone; it is carefully tied up
and put in sure keeping, so that it can only be brought out for
punishment. Sin and punishment are so inseparable that the
Hebrews could use the same word for both.

13. Israel could only win new life by being born again. But
the crisis had come and he refused to offer himself for repentance.
The **unwise son** is the foolish though unknowing child, that re-
fuses to do his part in a retarded birth, and the delay means death
for mother and child alike. It is a common Hebrew metaphor
(cf. 2 Kings xix. 3), and the coming of travail pangs gives the
further implication of the suddenness with which sorrow should
fall. Israel is here made to be first the mother and then the
child.

14 breaking forth of children. I will ransom them from the
power of the grave; I will redeem them from death: O
death, where are thy plagues? O grave, where is thy de-
15 struction? repentance shall be hid from mine eyes. Though
he be fruitful among his brethren, an east wind shall come,
the breath of the LORD coming up from the wilderness,
and his spring shall become dry, and his fountain shall be
dried up: he shall spoil the treasure of all pleasant vessels.
16 Samaria shall bear her guilt; for she hath rebelled against
her God: they shall fall by the sword; their infants shall
be dashed in pieces, and their women with child shall be
ripped up.

---

14. Earlier commentators take these words as a beautiful
promise that in the end all will be well. Certainly this is how
they are used by S. Paul (1 Cor. xv. 55), and the R.V. suggests
the same thing by taking the opening words **I will ransom them**
as a statement. It is true that elsewhere Hosea has transitions from
despair to hope which are no less violent than this one. But the
words are capable of an entirely different meaning, which accords
better with the rest of the passage, and editors are now agreed in
taking them not as a promise, but as an invoking of destruction
upon them, just as in ix. 14 the prophet prayed for the very thing
of which he warned them.

The following points are to be noted: (1) The two opening
sentences can be read as interrogatives, implying that God will
not save them. 'Shall I deliver them from the hand of Sheol?
Shall I redeem them from death?' (2) 'O Sheol, where are thy
plagues?' is really a summons to Sheol (the nether world) to come
and plague them. (3) The word translated **repentance** implies
being sorry at having to punish, and so virtually means 'pity.'
It is therefore a plain statement that God will *not* pity them

15. In spite of his flourishing condition, Israel shall be withered
up by the blast of Assyrian invasion coming from the east, which
shall be as the destroying breath of Jehovah Himself, and dry
up the land, for the foe will take away all that is precious to
them.

16. This final verse, which in the Heb. is the beginning of
ch. xiv., describes the impending fall of Samaria, which would be
accompanied by all the cruelties of barbarous warfare, and would
bring a ruin from which the city was destined never to recover.

F. God's love triumphs, in a new covenant with
His people. xiv. 1–9.

1–2. The prophet's final appeal to them to repent.

O Israel, return unto the LORD thy God; for thou hast **14**
fallen by thine iniquity. Take with you words, and return 2
unto the LORD: say unto him, Take away all iniquity, and
accept that which is good: so will we render *as* bullocks
the offering of our lips.

*3. They answer that henceforth they will trust in
God only.*

Asshur shall not save us; we will not ride upon horses: 3
neither will we say any more to the work of our hands, *Ye
are* our gods: for in thee the fatherless findeth mercy.

---

ch. xiv. One of the important questions connected with the
modern interpretation of Hosea relates to this chapter. The tendency has been to remove from his prophecies all that points
towards restoration or the promise of it. To those who have made
up their minds that he is a prophet of despair and not of hope,
there is no other course open than to reject ch. xiv. altogether as
a later addition. For the discussion of the question, see Introd.
pp. 19, 20.

1. The chapter is in the form of dialogue, the introduction
(*vv.* 1–2) being spoken by the prophet.

2. Take with you words. They had failed to find God because
their approach had been merely mechanical, and they only sought
Him 'with their flocks and with their herds' (v. 6). The voicing
of their heart's confession and resolve must be added to their
sacrifices. They must begin by simply asking for God's pardon, and
then resolving to offer their lips as readily as they offer their bullocks in sacrifice. The LXX rendering of 'the fruit of our lips,'
which has been explained as 'the sacrifice of praise and thanksgiving,' adds to the metaphor, but scarcely improves it.

3. They renounce their trust in foreign alliances, and in man-
made gods, believing that God's mercy is for those most in need.

we will not ride upon horses: cf. i. 7. Some would see here
a reference to Egypt, to whom they looked for aid with cavalry.

4-7. *Jehovah responds by assurance of forgiveness.*

4 I will heal their backsliding, I will love them freely : for
5 mine anger is turned away from him. I will be as the dew
   unto Israel : he shall blossom as the lily, and cast forth his
6 roots as Lebanon. His branches shall spread, and his
   beauty shall be as the olive tree, and his smell as Lebanon.
7 They that dwell under his shadow shall return ; they shall
   revive *as* the corn, and blossom as the vine : the scent
   thereof shall be as the wine of Lebanon.

8. *The dialogue ends with mutual resolves.*

8 Ephraim *shall say*, What have I to do any more with idols?

4-7. These verses are put into the mouth of God Himself, who
does not address Israel directly, but tells the prophet how He
will forgive them.

4. First the people are thought of individually, which is not
the usual feature of the book. It is **their** and **them.** But the
more familiar view follows in **him,** shewing again the solidarity
of the nation both in sin and in forgiveness.

5. A threefold simile is used to express the coming of God's
grace ; it revives like the night mist after the withering sirocco ;
it makes growth speedy and luxuriant like the blossoming of the
lily ; and its roots are firmer than those of flowers or trees, for
they strike downwards like those of the great mountain that raised
its snow-clad summit above the landscapes of northern Israel.

6. In the preceding verse the trees were omitted. Here the
picture is given of the spread of their branches (or 'saplings'),
while the olive with its constant foliage of silver-grey is one of
the beauties of the country. Moreover, the joy of Lebanon itself,
when it is closely approached, is in the scent of the pines which
cover its slopes.

7. The translation of this verse is uncertain. If **his** be right, it
seems to be the shadow of Jehovah Himself, who cannot therefore
be the speaker. In **they shall revive** *as* **the corn,** the word *as*
is not in the Hebrew, and some would render 'Once more they
that dwell under his shadow shall bring corn to life,' i.e. shall
cultivate the derelict fields. **the scent thereof** : the R.V. mg. is
better 'his memorial,' or rather 'his renown,' i.e. the fame of
Lebanon wine, which was known for its excellence.

8. It is not easy to allot these words to their respective speakers.
As the R.V. stands, Ephraim begins by a resolve finally to renounce idolatry. Jehovah replies that He has duly noted their

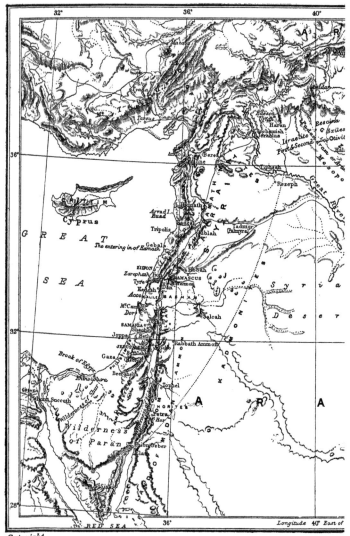

Copyright

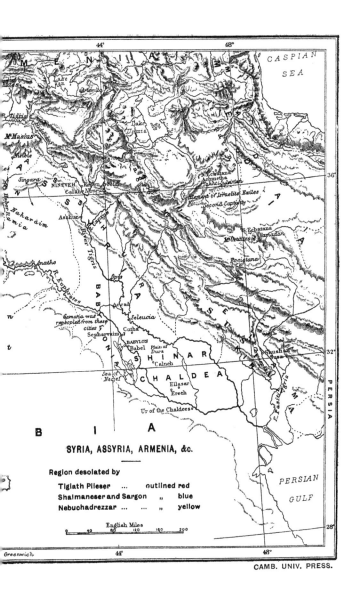

SYRIA, ASSYRIA, ARMENIA, &c.

Region desolated by

Tiglath Pileser ... ... outlined red
Shalmaneser and Sargon ,, blue
Nebuchadrezzar ... ... ,, yellow

English Miles
0   40   80   120   160   200

CAMB. UNIV. PRESS.

I have answered, and will regard him: I am like a green
fir tree; from me is thy fruit found.

9. *An epilogue, vindicating the ways of God.*

Who is wise, and he shall understand these things? prudent, 9
and he shall know them? for the ways of the LORD are
right, and the just shall walk in them; but transgressors
shall fall therein.

---

repentance. The nation, joyfully conscious of the new life of
grace, recognises in itself a growth like that of a young tree.
Finally, Jehovah reminds them that the fruit of the tree of
Ephraim (which bears the meaning of 'fruitfulness') comes from
Himself as Giver.

The whole of the verse may be Jehovah's; 'O Ephraim, what
etc.' as R.V. mg., or 'Ephraim—what hath he to do,' etc., as
LXX. Again, the words 'I am like a green fir tree' (or 'an ever-
green cypress') may be His own statement concerning Himself,
though it must be admitted that such a comparison of God to a
tree is quite unusual.

9. This final verse sounds like the comment of a later editor.
It makes the book of general application, as a message for all
ages. A right relation to God makes men move along the ways
of life; but those same ways may, if sin be persisted in, only
become 'an occasion of stumbling.'

INDEX

www.ingramcontent.com/pod-product-compliance
Ingram Content Group UK Ltd.
Pitfield, Milton Keynes, MK11 3LW, UK
UKHW020447010325
455719UK00015B/465